Lady Glenconner's Picnic Papers

and other Feasts with Friends

The Picnic Papers first published in 1983, by Hutchinson & Co. Ltd,
an imprint of the Hutchinson Publishing Group

This edition first published in the UK in 2024 by Bedford Square Publishers Ltd,
London, UK

bedfordsquarepublishers.co.uk
@bedsqpublishers

© Anne Glenconner, 2024

The right of Anne Glenconner to be identified as the author of this work
has been asserted in accordance with the Copyright, Designs and Patents Act 1988. All
rights reserved. No part of this book may be reproduced, stored in or introduced into
a retrieval system, or transmitted, in any form or by any means (electronic, mechanical,
photocopying, recording or otherwise) without the written permission of the publishers.

Any person who does any unauthorised act in relation to this publication
may be liable to criminal prosecution and civil claims for damages.
A CIP catalogue record for this book is available from the British Library.

A portion of the royalties from the sale of this book will be donated by the
author and the publisher to Safelives a registered charity in England and Wales
(Registered charity no. 1106864) to support their work to end domestic abuse.

ISBN
978-1-83501-241-3 (Paperback)
978-1-915798-87-9 (Hardback)
978-1-915798-88-6 (Trade Paperback)
978-1-915798-89-3 (eBook)

2 4 6 8 10 9 7 5 3 1

Typeset by Palimpsest Book Production Ltd, Falkirk, Stirlingshire

Printed in Great Britain by CPI Group (UK) Ltd, Croydon CR0 4YY

The manufacturer's authorised representative in the EU for product safety
is Easy Access System Europe, Mustamäe tee 50, 0621 Tallinn, Estonia
gpsr.requests@easproject.com

*To my friend Susanna who was
the inspiration for this book.*

Contents

Introduction	1
Princess Margaret – Picnic at Hampton Court	7
Roddy Llewellyn – Picnic at Glen	13
Susannah Constantine – Picnic Pandemonium	17
Angela Huth – The Perfect Picnic	21
Milton Gendel – Picnic in Rome	27
Harold Acton – A Picnic at the Ming Tombs	33
Dorothy Lygon – Picnics from the Past	41
Clementine Beit – Glory's Picnic	45
Jasper Guinness – Whoopee Picnic	49
James Lees-Milne – I Loathe Picnics	53
George and Gus Christie – Glyndebourne: A Critical View of the Picnic	59
Josceline Dimbleby – A Devonshire Picnic	65
Arabella Boxer – A Picnic for the Air	71
Margaret Vyner – Dominican Picnic	77
Mitch Crites – Picnics in India	83
Rupert Loewenstein – 'Caldo e Cremoso'	87
Bryan Adams – On the Road Houmous	91
Mary Hayley Bell – Picnic in China	93
Hugo Vickers – Garter Day Picnic	97

Colin Tennant – Mustique	101
Drue Heinz – A New England Clambake	105
Tina Brown – A Picnic at Macaroni Beach	113
Cecilia McEwan – Marchmont Picnic	117
Christabel and Jools Holland – A Cooling Water Picnic	120
Gaia Servadio – The Kingdom of Picnics	123
Rachel Johnson – Picnics and Scones	127
Susanna Johnston – Picnic at Bagni di Lucca	131
Tessa Baring – A Breakfast Picnic	135
Michael Grant – The Picnics of the Ancient Romans	139
Hugh Honour – A White Picnic	145
William Weaver – A Spontini Picnic	151
John Chancellor – A Country Churchyard Picnic	155
Clara Johnston – A Maharaja's Picnic Tea	161
Patrick Leigh Fermor – The Dales of Moldavia	165
Penelope Chetwode – Suprême de Volaille with St George in Cappadocia	171
Freya Stark – Dartmoor Picnic	177
Desmond Doig – When Abominable Snowmen Went Picnicking	179
Diana Cooper – Memories of Chantilly	183
John Julius Norwich – Sahara Picnics	187
Nicky Haslam – Some Enchanted Evening	193
Colette Clark – A Picnic in Portugal	197
Christopher Thynne – The Longleat Picnic	201
Derek Hill – A Painter's Picnic	205

Ian Graham – Picnic in Guatemala	209
Patrick Lindsay – Fourth of June Picnic	215
Min Hogg – Autumn Mushroom Picnic	219
Nicholas Coleridge – A Picnic at the Grange	223
Larissa Haskell – Russian Picnic	227
Valeria Coke – A Picnic by the Fountain of Perseus and Andromeda, Holkham, Norfolk	231
Sylvia Combe – A Picnic with the Poles	235
Elizabeth Leicester – Holkham Shooting Lunches	239
Anne Glenconner – Preparations for a Shooting Picnic at Holkham	243
Carey Basset – Carey's Cold Collation	249
Christopher Tennant – A Picnic with Boopa	253
Kelvin O'Mard – A Caribbean Picnic on Bequia	257
Mary Ann Sieghart – The Poacher's Pocket Picnic	263
Rupert Everett – Bird Island Picnic	267
Graham Norton – A Patch of Blue Sky	269
Lorraine Kelly – A Seaside Picnic	273
Gyles Brandreth – Let Them Eat Cake	277
Cliff Parisi – My Gi Tar Pik Nik	283
William Hanson – The Top Drawer Picnic	287
Picture Acknowledgements	291
Safelives	293
About the Author	295

Introduction

I am sadly writing this introduction on my own as Susanna Johnston, with whom I wrote the original *Picnic Papers*, died last year. I have missed her guiding hand on the new edition of this book but I hope she would approve.

Naturally, our undiluted gratitude went to the distinguished contributors who generously shared their picnicking experiences with us. Each and every one gave such encouragement by their enthusiasm and interest that the pleasure of corresponding, planning and talking with them over the venture was intense. Now I have a selection of new contributions to add to the mix and am equally grateful to today's writers for taking the time to share their memories and opinions of eating al fresco.

Susanna and I had both been dedicated picnickers since early youth and consequently find the subject of outdoor eating wholly absorbing. After all, it is a well-established habit. Our Stone Age forbears could be said to have picnicked after a fashion as they applied flint to firewood, culled berries, or sat with mammoth ribs in hand at the mouth of a cave; but whereas for them there was no alternative, for us there is all the excitement of the break away from daily ritual as we set out to find the perfect place to unpack the basket and perhaps even to find on-the-spot food to add to our provisions.

So – what is a picnic? The *Oxford English Dictionary* tells us in a few lines:

> *Picnic* Originally a fashionable and social entertainment in which each person present contributed a share of the provisions; now, a pleasure party including an excursion to some spot in the country where all partake of a repast out of doors... The essential feature was formerly the individual contribution; now it is the al fresco form of the repast.

Picnics, if the *Oxford English Dictionary* is to be trusted, were originally a foreign institution – an institution peculiar to the upper class; the *Annual Register* in 1802 declares that 'the rich have their sport, their balls, their parties of pleasure and their *pic-nics*' – and a year or two later James Beresford, in his popular work *The Miseries of Human Life, or The Last Groans of Timothy Testy and Samuel Sensitive: With a Few Supplementary Sighs from Mrs Testy,* describes one of his female characters as being 'full of Fete and Picnic and Opera'.

During the last hundred years or so picnicking has become such a popular pleasure that the phrase 'this is no picnic' is an accepted idiom to describe an unpleasant or unpopular experience. One of the joys of picnicking is proving how much depends on the setting and, cliché though it is, how much better something very ordinary can taste when eaten out of doors. In a bluebell wood with a campfire blazing, try making a dough of flour and water, add a pinch of salt and nothing else whatsoever. Roll it into a messy ball. Squeeze this lump onto the end of a long pointed stick. Thrust it into the flames and wait for it to turn brown. Here you have a 'damper' the time-honoured picnic delicacy. It is unlikely that it would be equally appreciated if served at a dining-room table by candlelight.

The very suggestion of a picnic tends to produce a strong reaction. Some people loathe them. Sir Steven Runciman, the historian, certainly appeared to disagree with the modern idea of picnicking as an enjoyable pastime. He told us in a letter:

> Memories crowd up of depression and discomfort; not quite dispelled by a picnic with Agatha Christie on Dartmoor, at which we drank champagne from silver goblets. Nor have my picnics been really eventful. I remember once picnicking on a Syrian roadside with a local colonel who had been sent to accompany me because I insisted on visiting a crusader castle near the Israeli frontier. Poor portly man, he had to climb to a mountaintop with me. And when we paused on the way back to eat, the Israelis took potshots at us from across the frontier, and the colonel, good Muslim though he was, consoled himself with the wine (local and awful) that I had brought with me. Or a picnic organised in Jericho (in 1931) by Abdul Hamid's retired astrologer, where Susanna's grandmother and I were poisoned. I have picnicked in a snowstorm on the Great Wall of China. In 1931, I picnicked, more happily, with a Rumanian prince on the (then) Bessarabian frontier, looking at suspicious Russian sentries across the river Dniester. That was happier, as was a picnic on a barge on the river Mekong where the royal band played Mozart. But on the whole my experiences have been a trifle *triste*.

However miserable the author of this letter may have been at the time of these ordeals, there can be no denying that his experiences were colourful. Some people feel that picnics are all very well when necessary, provided they are permitted to stick to the smudgy jam sandwich, hard-boiled egg and Bakelite teacup of their youth. We both look back on this type of picnic with nostalgia but never attempt to repeat it.

Some of those who have contributed to this book, Sir Harold Acton, for example, who was the first person to encourage us in this venture, have described unexpected and often nerve-racking adventures that have come about as the result of setting out on a picnic instead of allowing oneself to be securely tethered to a dining room or restaurant table. Some have shown how a day out of doors can be far more entertaining and educative, not to mention beneficial to one's purse, than one in a crowded pub.

Whatever our attitude, it remains a fact that we English, in the main, have an irresistible habit of eating al fresco, in spite of our unreliable climate. We will eat anywhere – in swamps, on haystacks, in sunshine, hail, fog or drizzle – anything to escape the routine of the kitchen table.

Not so for Graham Norton for whom 'planning a picnic is deciding to be disappointed'. For Graham, 'the only recipe anyone needs for a successful picnic is to see a patch of blue in the sky that is, as my father used to say, "big enough for a pair of sailor's trousers" and then pop into the nearest garage shop and stock up on some items packed with fat and salt. Consume these snacks somewhere you can at least see a tree and count yourself one of the luckiest people alive.'

I would like to thank Susanna's lovely daughters Clara, Lily, Rosy and Silvy who allowed me to refresh the original book and produce this new edition. I would also like to thank Johanna Tennant for being unfailingly kind and helpful – nothing is too much trouble, and for her encouragement and eagle eye. My darling daughters May and Amy were also invaluable in helping to bring the book up to date. Thanks to Sarah Harrison and Bedford Square Publishers for having faith in this book and giving me the wonderful opportunity for re-publishing it; thanks also to my agent Gordon Wise for being instrumental in bringing this book back to life. I would also like to thank the Queen who suggested SafeLives Charity which this book is supporting.

Princess Margaret

When we were first compiling this book, Susanna said how marvellous it would be if we could get Princess Margaret to write something for it. I wasn't at all sure she would, as she hadn't done anything like that before, but I broached the subject one evening when Princess Margaret and I were sitting in my Norfolk farmhouse. We'd had one or two whiskies, she liked to drink whisky after dinner, and I said, 'Ma'am there's something I'd like to ask you.' 'Yes, Anne what is it?' 'Well, you know Zanna and I are compiling a book of picnics with some proceeds going to the Glyndebourne Arts Trust?' She said, 'Anne you know I really hate opera.' Because she loved ballet, she knew a lot about it and was always going down to White Lodge, the Royal Ballet School in Richmond Park, and knew all the children there by name, but opera was not her thing. Anyway, she said, 'Well what are you going to ask me?' And I plucked up courage to ask if she could write a piece about a picnic for us and she simply said, 'Yes of course.'

Sometimes she surprised you, and then of course she came back to us with this lovely picnic at Hampton Court. That picnic was what she called one of her 'Treats', which every so often she would lay on for the members of the household, some of her ladies-in-waiting and some friends. Once she flew us to Osborne House on the Isle of Wight and we had a lovely picnic there. Another dinner she arranged for us was at the Tower of London, where they put a table in the midst of the Crown Jewels so we were surrounded by them, that was a great, great treat.

She loved organising these special occasions and being able to control the situation. It was similar when she used to come up to Glen, the house my husband Colin inherited in Scotland. When we were throwing a party, she'd often come the day before and help me with the flowers or check the dining-room table was laid properly. I'd show her the table plan and she'd say, 'Oh I'd love to sit next to so and so' she knew exactly what was going to happen. That was what she liked and it actually made her very easy. What she didn't like was going to someone's house and them not telling her anything, not knowing what the plan was. She hated surprises and that could make things difficult. I wonder if it was because she was going through a difficult time in her marriage, which she couldn't control, so she would want to be very exacting about those areas that she could. An example of this was that she knew precisely where everything was on her dressing table and would notice at once if something had been moved. She also collected shells and once a year one of my least favourite tasks was to wash them with soapsuds in a bath, dry them and put them back in the glass cupboards. I could never remember where they were supposed to go but she knew very precisely. 'Not there, Anne, can't you remember that one always goes there?' She was very particular like that.

Picnic at Hampton Court
HRH The Princess Margaret

Nearly all picnics in Britain end up in a lay-by by the road because, in desperation, no one can decide where to stop. I felt that another sort of treat, slightly different and rather more comfortable, was indicated. In my opinion picnics should always be eaten at table and sitting on a chair. Accordingly my picnic, in May 1981, took the form of an outing to Hampton Court.

This mysterious palace is like nothing else – very complex in structure and design. Built first by Cardinal Wolsey, it continued in construction through many reigns. One can wander through buildings dating from about 1514 to Charles II, William and Mary (with the help of Sir Christopher Wren), and George II. George III, when faced with the choice between it and Windsor Castle, mercifully chose the latter, as Hampton Court is rather like a haphazard village.

The Queen kindly let me take some friends. The best plan, it seemed to me, was to do some sightseeing and have lunch in the middle. So I got in touch with Sir Oliver Millar, Surveyor of the Queen's Pictures, who delighted in taking us round the recently restored Mantegnas, which are housed in their own Orangery. These were saved, happily, from the disastrous sale of Charles I's pictures by Cromwell, simply because Cromwell liked them.

I asked Professor Jack Plumb, Master of Christ's College, Cambridge, who had helped in writing the television series *Royal Heritage*, where we should best have our cold collation. He suggested the little Banqueting House overlooking the Thames. This seemed an excellent place for a number of reasons. It wasn't open to the public then, it was shelter in case of rain and, as far as anyone knew, there hadn't been a jolly there since the time of Frederick, Prince of Wales.

The Banqueting House used to be called the Water Gallery and was a retreat for Mary II. When she died William III pulled it down, because memories were too poignant, and built the Banqueting House on the same site. In the main room the walls and ceiling are by Verrio. The hall and anterooms are tiny, and being quite small it is nice and cosy. As three sides of it are surrounded by a sunken garden smelling warmly of wisteria and wallflowers, with the river flowing beneath its windows on the fourth side, it provided an ideal setting.

I took my butler to ensure that everything would be all right.

We started with smoked salmon mousse, followed by that standby of the English, various cold meats and beautiful and delicious salads. Those with room then had cheeses.

We drank a toast to Frederick, Prince of Wales and departed to inspect the famous old vine which has its own greenhouse and Nanny gardener. After that we wandered among the many visitors from abroad, round the lovely gardens and canals, viewing all the different façades of its many sides. We visited the chapel (redecorated by Wren) and the tennis court where we watched a game of royal or real tennis.

It was altogether a glorious day. The sun was shining on one of its brief appearances that summer, and everyone was happy.

Avocado Soup

- 3–4 avocado pears (depending on size)
- 1 pint (570 ml) chicken consommé
- ½ teaspoonful black pepper, salt and sugar mixed together

pinch of garlic salt
1 teaspoonful Worcestershire sauce
a little dry sherry
double cream

Put all the ingredients except the cream in blender. Leave in refrigerator for an hour or until cold. Serve in consommé cups with a little dab of double cream on each serving.

Roddy Llewellyn

Colin and I introduced Princess Margaret to Roddy Llewellyn, who I invited as an extra to a house party we were having at Glen. Princess Margaret was also a guest, and it was clear from day one that it was love at first sight, so I suppose it wasn't surprising that when I asked him to write about a picnic for our book he said, 'Well the very best picnics I ever had were at Glen.' Roddy became one of our very closest friends and he and Princess Margaret often came to stay at the Norfolk farmhouse I bought from my father when I got married. It became a safe haven for the two of them to escape all the awful press attention. Margaret would say to me, 'Roddy and I think your flower beds need weeding, Anne' and they would go out and weed side by side, kneeling on a weeding mat. It was one of the things she liked to do when she was here, like cleaning my car and insisting on always laying the fire for me. I wasn't allowed to touch the fire. 'I was a girl guide, Anne, you weren't, I know all about fires.' She'd fetch the wood from the basket in my hall and set about getting the fire going. She always sat on the chair next to the fire and when I'm here on my own I often feel that she's still here with me.

When Roddy left to get married, Princess Margaret decided that she was going to make friends with his wife, which we both did. She would load up the car with food and things she thought Roddy and darling Tania, his wife, and their gorgeous girls would like, standing at the boot and supervising what went in.

After her funeral, the Queen held a wake for Princess Margaret at Windsor. I was summoned to see the Queen and she said she wanted to thank me and Colin for giving Princess Margaret such a wonderful time in Mustique, and also for introducing her to Roddy. I thought that was so kind, as she really couldn't say anything like that at the time. I told Roddy about it and he was absolutely thrilled.

Picnic at Glen
Roddy Llewellyn

Style is something sadly lacking these days, but picnics at the Glen have more than their fair share of it. One magic day, several summers ago, the two main ingredients to ensure a successful luncheon picnic were there – sun and water. Delicious home-made pâtés, pies with thick crusts and galantines made possible the coming of *La Grande Bouffe* to Loch Eddy. Gin and tonics tinkling with ice mingled with the conversation, which often exploded into laughter. What seemed like an inexhaustible supply of chilled wine helped to wash down the kipper pâté and galantine of grouse, while huge bowls of salad were accompanied by a collection of stalwart cheeses which would have placated Mighty Mouse in his angriest mood. Lunch ended in a bonfire, a gentle row round Loch Eddy and a snooze on a rug or a walk. Whatever one did, one did it without a care in the world.

Kipper Pâté

> 7 oz (200 g) tin kipper fillets (preferably John West),
>   with most of the oil drained off
> 1 packet aspic, made up as instructions
> juice of half a large lemon
> 300 ml carton cream
> parsley for garnish

Put the kippers, ½ pint (275 ml) aspic (save a little for end), the lemon juice and cream in a liquidiser. When smooth put into an entrée dish and cool in the refrigerator for 45 minutes. Then cover with a little aspic. Decorate with parsley and eat with brown toast.

Galantine of Grouse

> 4 oz (110 g) calves' liver
> 8 oz (225 g) veal or sausage meat
> 1 lb (450 g) fat pork
> 4 rashers bacon
> a small bunch of chopped parsley
> 2 shallots
> 1 clove of garlic
> bay leaf
> breast of three grouse

Preheat the oven to gas mark 5 (375°F, 190°C). Put everything through the mincer except the bay leaf, bacon and grouse. Put the bay leaf at the bottom of the dish, then alternate layers of veal or sausage meat, grouse and bacon. Cook for about an hour then press down with a plate. Eat cold.

Susannah Constantine

I loved the television series Susanah presented with Trinny Woodall. *What Not to Wear* was a makeover show in the early 2000s which we were all glued to. But I really knew Susannah from the time when she was going out with Princess Margaret's son David Linley. They used to come out to Mustique and I always really liked her. She was devoted to Princess Margaret, it was something we shared. And Princess Margaret was very fond of Susannah, almost like a surrogate mother for her. Then, of course, she and David parted ways and I followed her career, but I only really reconnected with her recently when she sent me her memoir to read. She is always so friendly and nice and we enjoy reminiscing about Princess Margaret when we meet.

Picnic Pandemonium
Susannah Constantine

I was never a fan of picnics and have mostly lied about how much I enjoy eating in the great outdoors. It's not the unpredictable weather, uninvited insects, dribbled ketchup or accidental mouthfuls of sand that put me off, but the work it takes to pull a picnic together. Usually a drive, walk or sail away, you can't afford to leave anything behind and if you do, the picnic is a failure. You can't have more than one person at the helm for this reason. Too many cooks leave too much room for error.

I have been on picnics where everything has arrived and been beautifully prepared and packed by a silver-fingered cook. Picnics on Macaroni Beach in Mustique with Princess Margaret were always an event to relish, and I have many happy memories of Ma'am presiding at the end of a pop-up plastic table. But this was because I wasn't accountable for not forgetting any number of 'the most important' ingredients.

We have a home on the Helford River in Cornwall. It's been in the family eons and as anyone who has holidayed in the UK knows – it's impossible to avoid picnicking. Resentfully I've *had* to embrace this very British of traditions.

Being extraordinarily greedy and a bit of a foodie I can't bring myself to lighten the workload with bought sandwiches and a packet of crisps. I'm not a nutritional snob. I'll eat anything, but one of the primary ways I like to show my family love is through food. And cooking is one of the few things I'm better at than my husband Sten.

Whatever the season or temperature it's always the same. Chipolata sausages. Home-made garlic mayonnaise and crispy parmesan chicken nuggets. Roasted new potatoes with rosemary. Carrot and cucumber batons, hummus. Tunnock's Teacakes for pudding. Lots of greaseproof paper, tinfoil and Tupperware. The menu doesn't change but the venue does and while you don't expect a picnic to come with danger to life, our best and most memorable involved torrential rain, huge waves and an almost-upturned boat.

★

It was a calm and beautiful morning when we set off. A gentle breeze nudged our Rib from its mooring packed with cold box, portable barbecue, three small children and a dog called Archie. Health and Safety has never been a strong point in our family, and we thought not a lot as the wind picked up. By the time we approached Porthbeor beach near St Mawes in an ever-increasing swell, it became clear we had been caught out in a squall with gusts reaching 60 mph. Approaching the beach we were reduced to a crawl, battling huge, cold waves and crashing white water. If ever our ex-RNLI Rib was going to capsize it was now. With the surf breaking we were all tossed off the rubber sides but managed stay onboard. Archie fell out and between waves my husband screamed. 'Jump now!'

Soaked, scared and in peril of losing our picnic I seized the food, threw as much as I could on to the sand and yelled at the kids to grab on to me. We all survived unhurt. There is nothing like adrenalin to boost an appetite. Our picnic never tasted better, and we have never forgotten the day 'we *nearly* drowned'.

Angela Huth

When Angela was pregnant and bedridden, she writes about how Princess Margaret used to go over to her house with Tony (Armstrong-Jones) on a Saturday evening with a delicious cold supper, including the china and the glasses, and Tony would set up a film in the bedroom which they would all watch together. Angela was a close friend of Princess Margaret, which was how I got to know her, and we often used to go and stay with her and her husband in Oxford where he was a don. She was a novelist who wrote among others a terrific book called *Land Girls*, which was turned into a film starring Rachel Weisz. Her story about Princess Margaret shows how thoughtful she could be. I remember when I was having a very difficult time with my two older boys and then Christopher had his terrible accident, she would constantly phone up to see if I was all right and would send a car to pick me up and bring me to Kensington Palace for lunch. She'd say, 'Anne you've got to eat you know, you've got to keep your strength up – for Christopher's sake.' She was incredibly kind like that, which I don't think is something many people know about her.

The Perfect Picnic
Angela Huth

There are picnics of the mind and picnics in real life. Most people have experienced both and know the difference between them.

In the imagination the *déjeuners sur l'herbe* which we attend seem to be very similar. There is always warmth, but cool shade, iced white wine, grass that doesn't prickle, butterflies – a veritable Impressionist picture, happily out of focus. If the imagination were unkind enough to look closer, the dream would be broken.

In reality the dream is broken, almost inevitably, as soon as the very idea of a picnic is cast abroad, and the hamper packed. (Hamper indeed: where are the hampers of yesteryear, those magnificent wicker baskets, lids slotted with knives and forks, and stacked with their special plates? It is supermarket cool boxes in which we pack our feasts of today, and they are not at all the same.)

But disillusionment is of no matter to the determined picnicker. Once launched on the expedition, he blooms with optimism however black the cloud that billows from nowhere, however large the spots of rain. On, on he drives past those Picnic Areas whose corrugated lavatories and official rustic tables make him sad to think this generation of townsfolk think *they* are proper picnic places. On to a small stretch of balding coast with a misted view over a grim sea. The wind might die down, but until it does where better to eat than the stuffy cosiness of the car, thick with the smells of melons, cheese and wet dogs? Children shriek, there's strawberry jam on the steering wheel and, by heavens, it's almost the fun we had imagined.

For there is probably no hardier race of picnickers than the British. On Bodmin Moor I have watched summer sleet sizzle the flames of the barbecue on which lie dozens of drenched *langoustines*, where in a nearby bowl *fraises du bois* turn to pulp. But the smiles of the crowd gathered under their anoraks wavered not. I have seen members of the edge-of-the-motorway brigade sprayed black with mud by passing cars as they enjoy their sliced-bread sandwiches. I have seen trainspotters relishing Chinese takeaways on a stack of mailbags at Paddington Station on a November afternoon.

But happily, whatever the disappointment of real-life picnics, in retrospect it is the delights that are remembered. And thus our nostalgia for picnics. We continue to persevere with them, for when they work they are occasions of particular pleasure.

My own first memories of picnic life were at the age of twelve: curried egg sandwiches at sunless Overstrand. My sister and I – scoffing at our parents' tweed coats and mackintoshes. Eight years later there were picnic lunches at point-to-points in Hampshire – occasions of supreme sophistication, those. The backs of Land Rovers were let down to reveal the last of the real hampers of delicious food. I don't remember precisely *what* food. I have no recollection of quiches in those mid-fifties days – they were to become fashionable much later. But I do remember sturdy wicker baskets with separate compartments for bottles of drink, and standing round with tiny glasses in fuzzy-gloved hands, sipping cherry brandy and sloe gin against the cold.

The point of those picnics was not, of course, the food (or even the horses) but the chance to brush against the fancied member of the opposite sex and be offered a sausage on a stick with a look of such penetrating desire that the legs would tremble in the gumboots like grass in a wind. How beautiful they were, those sporting young men in their riding macs that clacked like a field of cabbages when they moved – their greenish trilbies cocked saucily over one eye, their incredible eyelashes, and small patches of mysteriously long hair on their cheeks. No wonder the contents of the hampers were of no consequence.

But of all memorable picnics the one nearest to perfection of imaginary picnics took place in Cornwall four years ago. It was the inspiration of those master picnickers, Marika and Robin Hanbury-Tenison. She was one of our finest cooks. He is a renowned explorer. They have feasted off rattlesnakes and spiders in many a foreign jungle in their time, but at home on Bodmin Moor their picnics were incomparable.

It was May, very warm. We were asked to wear Edwardian clothes, and to meet in the bluebell woods. These woods were sprawled about along a valley – crumbling old trees, lichen-covered – their frizz of new leaves a-dazzle with spring sun. Our chosen place was on the mossy banks of a stream: a place where wild thyme grew. Tables were laid with damask cloths and spread with a feast in keeping with the Edwardian era. We lay on cashmere rugs, crushing bluebells. We ate iced strawberry soup, chicken and bacon pie, cherries in wine and pyramids of meringues. Suddenly through the trees came our elegant Ambassador to Japan, Sir Fred Warner. He wore a blazer, straw boater and almond-pink silk tie. Behind him rustled his wife, Simone, in forget-me-not blue, who sang to us in her clear piping voice while her small sons fell in and out of the stream. There will never be another picnic like that middle-aged frolic in the bluebell woods, but there will be others of surprising and enchanting character, and in old age we perennial picnickers will still be there, sharing the present delight beneath umbrella or parasol, remembering all the while the hampers of our youth.

Strawberry Soup

- 2 chicken stock cubes
- 1 pint (570 ml) water
- 2 lb (900 g) fresh or frozen strawberries
- ½ teaspoon mixed herbs
- salt, pepper
- ½ teaspoon ground ginger
- 1 small carton natural yoghurt
- 2 tablespoons finely chopped chives

Combine the chicken stock cubes and water, bring to the boil and stir until the cubes are dissolved. Add the strawberries and herbs, season with salt and pepper, and mix in the ground ginger. Bring to the boil again, simmer for 5 minutes and then rub through a fine sieve to remove the seeds. Stir in the yoghurt, mix until smooth, and serve hot or iced with a garnish of chopped chives.

Milton Gendel

Milton, an American Italian art critic and photographer, lived in what was described as 'The most wholly desirable house in Rome.' The Palazzo Pierloni Caetani was situated on the Isola Tiberina, a little island in the middle of the Tiber river. I do remember it was very damp. He had been introduced to Princess Margaret's best friend Judy Montagu by the British socialite Lady Diana Cooper, and they were married in 1962. Judy was a very old friend of my husband Colin, and we often went to stay with them, as did Princess Margaret. It was one of Princess Margaret's favourite stops in Italy along with La Pietra which was the home of Harold Acton, which we also visited. Milton and Judy had a little girl, Anna, who had a total of twenty-four very well-chosen godparents, one of whom was Princess Margaret. When Judy died very suddenly at the age of forty-nine, Princess Margaret stepped in and invited Milton and Anna to the royal palaces during the summer when Anna was on school holiday. Milton always had a camera on him and was constantly snapping away, I think because he was always around the royal family he got intimate relaxed photographs of them. He took a rather wonderful one of the Queen wearing a headscarf preparing burgers to feed her dogs at Balmoral. When he asked if he could take one more photograph she apparently replied, 'Well, I'll be very surprised if you've got any more film left.'

Picnic in Rome
Milton Gendel

For generations the English have been domesticating the Sublime by choosing its precincts for their picnics. There is no beauty spot in creation, on Alp, lakeside or riverbank, in jungle or desert, that has not served as a setting for a group of English people with picnic baskets, spirit lamps and teapots in cosies. At least this was so before the highway picnic became current, with picnickers on folding chairs and the open boot of the car serving as buffet.

Once, in the spring, a few decades ago, Rome offered a happy conjunction of scenic sublimity and picnicking English to provide appropriate foreground figures. Evelyn Waugh, in the Holy City for his annual Easter devotions, was the star of the occasion. Jenny Crosse, daughter of Robert Graves and correspondent of *Picture Post*, was always the moving spirit on such occasions. She rang up Babs Johnson, the writer known as Georgina Masson.

'Evelyn Waugh is here with Diana Cooper – you know – she's Mrs Stitch in his novels. I thought we might have it at your place.'

The self-educated daughter of an Indian Army officer, Babs brought the competence, pertinacity and inspiration of a Mrs Beeton to her various interests. The two ladies devised the guest list, which contained enough flannel-coated men and hatted or bandanna-ed women to provide the cast for a proper English picnic.

Then Evelyn Waugh announced that he would come to the picnic only if he did not have to sit on the ground. With some regret Babs Johnson gave up the thought of the remoter romantic glades of the villa, where daffodils were springing and cherry trees blossoming, and moved her tables and chairs out in front of the vaulted stable that old Prince Filippo Doria let her have as a grace-and-favour home in his park.

A lovely limpid blue and gold April day framed Babs's stableyard rock garden. Jenny bustled about serving Frascati, mascarpone and ricotta seasoned with salt and pepper and garnished with a sprinkling of paprika. Next came tufted raw fennel, to be pulled apart and dipped in olive oil with mustard, and eggs stuffed with anchovies. Round loaves of crusty bread, the descendants of those found – baked hard – in the ashes of Pompeii, were set out together with plates of prosciutto, minuscule slices of spicy salami, rounds of lonza and mortadella.

When Evelyn Waugh arrived he was allotted a little table to himself where he sat plump with a commanding air, more lordly than any rank-proud gentleman on the Grand Tour.

The talk turned on the personality and history of Pius XII, the reigning pontiff. Jenny and Babs were censorious. The Pope was austere, autocratic. Sympathetic to German *Kultur*, he had not been outspoken enough against the Nazis. True, the Vatican had contributed to the gold ransom extorted from the Roman Jews during the German occupation, but it hadn't prevented their deportation or the massacre of the hostages at the Fosse Ardeatine. A devout Catholic guest blushed with discomfiture at the protracted and irreverent discussion. Evelyn Waugh, now impatient, banged his fork on the table.

Jenny placatingly held out a bottle of Frascati.

'Some wine, Evelyn?' He fixed her with a cold blue eye. 'Mrs Crosse,' he said, with compelling emphasis, 'has anyone ever remarked on the uncanny resemblance between you and the late unlamented Mrs Roosevelt? Undoubtedly she was one of the most ill-favoured women the world has ever seen.'

A stunned silence followed this pronouncement, as its author returned to spearing rounds of salami. It was broken by Diana Cooper, out of the depths of her bonnet: 'He's just *too* awful.'

Jenny retreated to the stable converted into a sitting-room where Babs was uncorking some wine. 'Are you crying?' Babs asked. Jenny repeated what had just been said to her. Babs, a sturdy woman with iron-grey hair, a determined look and a kind eye, listened with growing indignation. She had been brought up near the Khyber Pass, where respect was paid to the New Testament on Sundays and holidays, but where daily life was ruled more by the Old Testament. She was also uncompromising in her view of women's rights.

'Jenny,' she said, 'you go right out there now and hit him as hard as you can. You're a woman and he won't dare hit you back.' Jenny looked shocked, but obediently turned and went back to the rock garden.

Evelyn Waugh peered up at her with a bland expression as she addressed him: 'Evelyn, I have always admired you as a writer. After your behaviour today I want you to know that I no longer admire you as a man. But, as Christians, perhaps we meet on common ground. So I *forgive* you.'

As a master of dry comedy he must have relished the turning of his elective worm into a monument of moral dignity. The company certainly did: there were shouts of laughter, followed by praise for Jenny and belated reproval for Evelyn Waugh.

'I don't care much for picnics,' said Waugh when it was time to go. 'But I enjoyed this one immensely. And I shall never forget it.'

Anchovy Eggs

- eggs
- mayonnaise
- anchovy fillets
- salt
- pepper
- lemon juice
- mustard
- cayenne
- basil

Hard-boil the eggs. Crack the shells and drop immediately into cold water to minimise the darkening of the yolks. Shell and cut in halves lengthwise. Mash the yolks and moisten with mayonnaise and well-pounded anchovy fillets. Season to taste with salt, pepper, lemon juice, mustard and cayenne. Refill the whites with this mixture and sprinkle with chopped basil.

Harold Acton

Harold Acton might well have been at the picnic described by Milton Gendel, as he was a great friend of Evelyn Waugh. An art historian, novelist and poet, he was said to be the inspiration for the character of Anthony Blanche in *Brideshead Revisited*. Villa la Pietra, just outside Florence where he lived, was Princess Margaret's other favourite place to stay in Italy. I used to go and stay at this exquisitely beautiful villa with her. 'Come on, Anne,' Princess Margaret would say to me, 'we've got to be well behaved here,' and she was. People used to be desperate for an invitation to lunch, they knew Harold loved good caviar, which cost a bomb, so they would phone up and say they had a present for him and could they pop in... there was quite a lot of that going on. But as we arrived he would always be standing on the steps to greet us: 'Ma'am welcome to my humble abode, which is at your disposal.' Princess Margaret used to give me a look and I'd get the giggles and she'd tell me off for laughing. The house really was magical, it was full of wonderful paintings, the sheets were all of the finest linen and he had just the right amount of divine soap and bath essence in the bathrooms, which he had specially made. Harold was a wonderful conversationalist, you really had to be on form when you saw him, but I felt honoured to have known him and of course delighted to have him in the book.

A Picnic at the Ming Tombs
Harold Acton

The Tuscan countryside has been amenable to picnics since the fifteenth century, when Lorenzo the Magnificent invited his cronies to rustic repasts in the bosky Mugello and in cool Camaldoli. Cured ham and pungent cheese stimulated a thirst for the vintages celebrated in Francesco Redi's dithyrambic *Bacchus in Tuscany*, which in turn stimulated a flow of rhyme and melody. Lorenzo's best poems are redolent of picnics.

The more refined cakes and sandwiches of my childhood were consumed with appetites sharpened by climbs up Vincigliata or Monte Morello, and by games of hide-and-seek and blind man's buff, but I remember the delicious cakes better than the company. We lounged on the grass as in Manet's *Déjeuner sur l'herbe*, though none of the girls reclined naked in our midst, for we were strictly supervised by a governess. Since nothing more sensational occurred than a bleeding nose or a bruised knee, my memory of those bygone picnics is hazy.

The neighbourhood of Beijing where I spent seven happy years, was even more amenable to picnics. A novel called *Peking Picnic* was popular at the period, but I forget if the title was justified by the contents. Picnics, however, were traditional in ancient China, whose greatest poets considered wine essential to the enjoyment of nature. Many a Chinese scroll depicts parties of poetical tipplers in a secluded spot among mountains and bamboo groves.

The Western Hills near Beijing were often chosen for al fresco meals, but after the Japanese invasion it was deemed foolhardy to venture far from the city, since roving bandits and marauding soldiery infested the countryside. The Ming Tombs, for instance, twenty miles north-west of Beijing, were officially out of bounds.

A spirited American lady, whom I shall call 'Mrs Schooner', was determined to take the risk before returning to Massachusetts, and she invited me to join her for a picnic at the Tombs, perhaps because she could find no other escort. She told me she had hired a motor car with some difficulty by paying the driver through the nose. 'He's a cutie but he's kinda yaller. He was even scared of taking me to the Summer Palace.'

Unwilling to appear pusillanimous, I agreed to accompany her to the Valley of Thirteen Tombs. She knew no Chinese, whereas I was fairly fluent in the language. Though she was double my age she had twice my energy: her enthusiasm for everything she saw was infectious. The hired car was filled with a rich variety of edibles from the Hôtel de Pékin where she was staying. She told me she was bringing foie gras as well as smoked eel and half a dozen bottles of Pouilly. 'I won't let you starve, dear. You are a good sport to keep me company. All the others I invited made some lame excuse, the darned cissies!'

Mrs Schooner whooped with laughter as we set off from the hotel. 'Wouldn't it be fun if we were kidnapped by bandits?' she said gaily. She was dressed and made up as for a morning's shopping in Bond Street – an invitation to rapine, I thought, in spite of her certain age. The road was so bumpy that she clung to me when we swerved past a file of camels. By fits and starts she related her life history. 'At high school I was a champion wrestler and I've had four husbands to wrestle with. None of them gave me the love a girl expects: they were more interested in my dollars. I had a hunch that I'd find my fifth in China, that's why I'm here. So far nothin' doin'... '

She talked so much that I was distracted from the scenery – a sweeping bare plain dotted with burial mounds and an occasional stele. The October weather was serene, the sky like Venetian glass.

After an hour my hostess said, 'I'm getting thirsty, dear, what about you? Let's stop the car for a nip of dry martini. It's in the big thermos flask.' So the driver stopped near a file of donkeys, loaded with panniers and bundled blue figures on top of them. Nothing if not democratic, she filled a glass for the driver, but he said '*Pu kan*' ('I dare not'), so she offered him some chewing gum and swallowed his portion herself.

Apart from the donkeys the road was deserted. 'How far have we still to go? For twenty miles it seems more like a hundred. I'm glad I brought plenty of nourishment.'

I heartily agreed, for her incessant monologue had become wearisome. The car jogged along almost as slowly as the donkeys and by the time we approached a white marble *p'ai-lou*, or ceremonial gateway, Mrs Schooner announced, 'I'm famished. Let's hop out and eat!' As a magnificent pavilion was visible yonder, I proposed that we should stop there. It contained a huge stone tortoise supporting a memorial tablet. Its massive coral-red walls and yellow-tiled double roof against a background of rippling lapis lazuli hills were as impressive as any in the Forbidden City.

'Okay,' said Mrs Schooner. We spread a rug on a patch of coarse grass and unpacked the baskets of victuals with enough glasses and cutlery for at least half a dozen people. 'The situation is pretty but it sure is lonesome,' Mrs Schooner remarked, peering through her binoculars.

'Well, what did you expect? This is where the Ming emperors of the last truly Chinese dynasty were buried with their wives and concubines.'

'It doesn't look like a cemetery to me. Have we come to the right place?'

Certainly the Valley of Thirteen Tombs had nothing akin to the cluttered cemeteries of Europe and America. It was all too grandiose: its monumental buildings were still brightly coloured though decayed, and the landscape was on too vast a scale. No soul was in sight. One was reminded of the Egyptian pyramids and of Shelley's 'Ozymandias': 'Look on my works, ye Mighty, and despair!'

'I guess I'd have liked to be an imperial concubine,' Mrs Schooner mused aloud. 'They must have had loads of fun without responsibilities.'

'I doubt it, for they had jealous wives to contend with. Many were poisoned or drowned in wells.'

'Don't talk of poison, this pâté's yummy. A pity we can't make toast here. Just spread it on a cracker.'

While I was drawing the cork from a bottle of wine, three ragged men with guns appeared suddenly from nowhere. 'Bandits,' said our terrified driver and scampered off. The men sauntered up and stared at us while we were eating. They stared as if they had never seen 'foreign devils' before. Robust, with high cheekbones and ruddy complexions, they were typical northerners of peasant stock. 'I guess the boys are hungry,' Mrs Schooner remarked. 'Hi there!' she called, offering them some of our chicken and ham and buttered rolls. 'Ask them to sit down and introduce themselves.'

When I spoke to them their faces lit up with broad grins. They sat cross-legged beside us with their battered guns, and once they had sampled our fare they ate like ravenous tigers. Our knives and forks perplexed them; accustomed to chopsticks, they preferred to eat with their fingers. They dangled the layers of fat on the ham above their open mouths and swallowed with a noise of trickling water.

Though they were not very communicative, I gathered that they were disbanded soldiers, irregulars who had been fighting the Japanese, whom they ironically referred to as 'dwarf bandits'. Now they intended to make their way home to villages in the north. Concerning ourselves they were inquisitive. 'How old are you? Are you husband and wife? Where do you come from and what is your honourable country?' – the usual questions. Our wine had less appeal for them than the cocktails, but they soon polished off the food. Not a scrap was left for our driver. 'Serve him darn well right for leaving us in the lurch!' was Mrs Schooner's comment.

'*Tsamen tou shih p'êng-yu*' ('We're all friends'), the men repeated, and they belched appreciatively. One of them, flushed with dry martinis, fired his gun into the air to demonstrate his gratitude.

'Supposing they all start shooting? I guess they're trigger-happy.' Mrs Schooner betrayed slight alarm through her tough veneer. 'Now we've seen a few live bandits, why bother to see the Tombs?'

The men thanked us with formal courtesy, bowing and shaking their own hands. I distributed a few coins for their journey money and we wished each other *I lu p'ing-an*, a safe and peaceful return. Our driver slunk back rather crestfallen as soon as they were out of sight. 'You were in luck. They could have shot you,' he said. 'And I could have shot them,' said Mrs Schooner, producing a pocket pistol from her leather bag.

Having come so far with that definite intention, I was anxious not to miss the Triumphal Way leading to the Tombs, but Mrs Schooner had had enough. 'I'm disappointed in the bandits,' she declared. Already she was bored and grumpy. Her subconscious had yearned for a shindy, a little bloodshed. I left her with the driver to finish the wine and relax while I wandered towards the avenue of statues in the distance. Very strange they looked, standing in couples on that desolate plain. Sculptured lions, horses, camels, griffins, unicorns, elephants, civil and military officials over life-size carved from single blocks of stone, the elephants thirteen-feet high and fourteen-feet long, formed a perpetual guard of honour for the funeral procession of dead emperors.

'You really ought to see the statues,' I urged Mrs Schooner. 'They are quite extraordinary if not unique. Do let me take you there.'

'Nuts to statues. I've a cocktail engagement at the embassy and my thermos flask is empty.'

The actual Tombs were ahead of us and I was sorry not to visit that of Yung Lo, the founder of modern Beijing. But Mrs Schooner was stubbornly deaf to persuasion. On the way back she was silent and comatose, to my intense relief. Perhaps I was not the right companion for such a picnic. Later I heard that she had spread a romantic report of our carousal with wild bandits armed to the teeth. The remaining bottles of Pouilly were sent to my house with a note of farewell on pink writing paper with a silver monogram: 'When you come to Magnolia, I'll give you a proper picnic. Wombs not tombs, and barbecues on the beach. *Aloha*, as they say in Hawaii, Sincerely, Arabella Schooner.'

Dorothy Lygon

The character of Cordelia Flyte in *Brideshead Revisited* was said to have been inspired by Dorothy Lygon. She had been brought up at Maddresfield Court in Worcestershire and was known as one of the 'bright young things' of the 1930s. Evelyn Waugh was a friend and regular visitor to the house who knew Dorothy as 'Poll'. Dorothy ended up briefly marrying the somewhat uncontroversial Robert Heber-Percy who had been the lover of the composer Lord Berners. Berners was very eccentric and lived in a house near Susanna, I remember he had lots of doves and dyed them all different colours. Not surprisingly the marriage didn't last very long and they split up after about a year. Heber-Percy had a housekeeper who was in love with him and she saw Dorothy off pretty smartly.

Picnics from the Past
Dorothy Lygon

Picnics played a definite part in our lives when we were young. They fell into two categories – nursery outings, which were ordinary nursery teas taken to the garden, the woods or the beach, or family picnics, which were rarer and more elaborate, often including some of the household. I remember one of the latter sort on a steamer on the River Severn and another by the weir on the Teme. A third was on the Goodwin Sands, off the Kent coast, large areas of which are uncovered during the extreme tides of spring and autumn. The remains of a German submarine wrecked there during the 1914–1918 war were still visible in the 1920s; the sand was quite firm to walk on as long as there was no water on it, otherwise it shifted round one's feet and started to engulf them in a way that was both frightening and exciting.

The food on these grown-up picnics was always the same, but they didn't happen often enough for us to get bored with it. There were bridge rolls filled with Russian salad, small mutton pies known as Buckingham Palace pies, jam puffs and coffee and chocolate éclairs. The mutton pies were particularly good. There was no need for knives, forks or spoons and I can't remember any being provided. I think we drank lemonade; the men would have had beer or whisky or cider – certainly not wine, nor do I remember ice. For a later recipe the following is one which has evolved over the last year or two; it can be used for sandwiches (made with brown bread well buttered), or put in small ramekins or cartons to eat on its own.

Dorothy's Russian Salad

Allow 1½ eggs per person if the eggs are large, or 2 if small. Hard-boil them and, after peeling, chop roughly and tip them into a roomy bowl. Add salt, pepper, a good sprinkle of Worcestershire sauce and enough single cream to moisten the mixture. Next add herbs, some kind of onion (either chives cut with scissors or spring onions or minced shallots), then parsley and/or whatever you have available – dill, chervil, tarragon and fennel are all good. Sometimes I have added chopped shrimps or prawns quite successfully. It can be made in advance and kept under cling film or foil in the refrigerator. I have not tried freezing it, but have found it a good flexible basic recipe.

Buckingham Palace Pies

>   short pastry
>   1½ lb cooked mutton, beef, chicken or rabbit
>   2 shallots, finely chopped
>   butter
>   stock
>   rich brown gravy
>   salt, pepper and Worcestershire sauce
>   beef jelly

Preheat the oven to gas mark 7 (425°F, 220°C). Make a number of tartlet cases with the short pastry. Cut out two circles, one smaller than the other, for the tops of the tartlets. Fit the larger circles into a greased mince pie tin, which usually makes 12 cases. Cut a hole in the smaller of the circles. Bake blind until lightly browned.

Cut slices of cooked meat into small squares, rejecting any fat or sinew. Cook two finely chopped shallots in butter and mix with the meat in a pan with enough stock to cover it. It should then be cooked slowly for about an hour until the meat is extremely tender. Remove the meat, cover with a good rich brown gravy seasoned with salt, pepper and a dash of Worcestershire sauce, and fill the cases with this mixture. Put a little meat jelly on the top, cover with the pastry circles, one on top of the other, and fill the hole with beef jelly.

Mamie's Comfort

Fill a large thermos with hot Bovril mixed to required strength and lace generously with port and brandy. A very useful hot drink for a cold picnic.

Clementine Beit

Being tied up and robbed by the IRA is happily not an everyday occurrence but it was something that happened to Clementine Beit. She was a cousin of the famous Mitford sisters and was married to Sir Alfred Beit who had inherited an incredible art collection including works by Goya, Velasquez and Gainsborough. They bought a Palladian house just outside Dublin called Russborough, partly to house all their marvellous paintings. Of course, people knew about it, and one day an IRA gang led by the heiress Rose Dugdale broke into the house when they were all at home. Everyone was tied up and nineteen paintings were stolen. Eventually the police turned up and freed Alfred. Two hours later, as he was telling them which paintings had been taken, they asked him if Lady Beit had been at home. 'Oh god, yes she was!' he said. He'd totally forgotten about her! Eventually they found her in the cellar bound and gagged. I think she'd been mouthy and annoyed them, which is why they'd dumped her in there.

We knew the Beits through parties and the social scene in London and I became one of a group of ladies Alfred used to take out to events and play tennis with. It was after I was married, but Colin was often in Mustique and Clementine was thrilled to have a break, so was delighted when we used to go off with Alfred for an afternoon. Despite being enormously rich he was very careful with his money. If we went to Wimbledon we used to have to cut the order of play out of the newspaper so he didn't have to buy a programme, and bring our own cushions so he didn't have to hire them. We were allowed strawberries, or ice cream or coffee but not all three.

They didn't have any children and Clementine adored her dog so it was totally fitting that she wrote about a dog picnic for us.

Glory's Picnic
Clementine Beit

Our Ridgeback dog, Glory, loved picnics. He always seemed to know when one was being planned and would get into the car when he saw that it was about to be loaded up; everything was then packed around him and we would set off. On arrival at the picnic spot, he would sit and watch the baskets being unpacked, drooling with anticipation. We always took his dinner with us, and when he had wolfed it down he would do the rounds, pleading with everyone that he was still starving. There were never any scraps left to tidy away before leaving if Glory had been on a picnic!

Glory's Picnic Pudding

Spread 3 or 4 slices of bread – preferably brown – with dripping or butter, including the brown jelly from your dripping bowl if possible. Chop up some scraps and leftovers, mince (raw or cooked), and a little chopped or grated cheese (if liked by dog). Chicken skin was much liked. Cut the slices of bread into fairly small squares. Put alternative layers of bread and scraps into the dog's bowl, moisten with warm gravy or Oxo and mix up lightly with a fork – the mixture should not be too soggy. Cover the bowl with foil.

In Africa we always took water for Glory.

Jasper Guinness

Jasper's party trick was to go into an Italian bar and drink the entire top shelf! He did like a drink, and picnics could never be too far from the house as inevitably many of the guests would end up unable to stand and having to crawl back. He was also a Mitford – his grandmother was Diana Mitford, and his mother, Ingrid was one of my closest friends. I adored Jasper, who tragically died at the age of 57. He lived in Italy with his wife Camilla with whom he bought and did up a glorious Tuscan villa, Arniano. Camilla is an interior designer and we used to talk about Indian fabrics as Colin and I always dressed in Indian clothes that we'd brought back from our trips there. I urged her to go to India to buy materials, which she did. In the process of creating the beautiful garden at Arniano, Jasper discovered a real love of plants and became a botanist, teaching himself landscape garden design. He went on to design other gardens for the great and the good in Tuscany. His sense of fun shines through in his Whoopee picnic.

Whoopee Picnic
Jasper Guinness

Nothing I like more than a picnic. Easily planned, but when the day dawns, I find, one does not always feel exactly one's best. But it's 'yoydleoy' and down to the market we go. First stop: the butcher. I've always been fond of spare ribs, unlike the Italians. They don't set much store by them and, as a result, they damn near give them away. The key word is '*rosticciana*'. Then off to the greengrocer for potatoes, lettuce, tomatoes, lemons and, most important, a huge watermelon (*cocomero*).

Now, as Sherlock's friend asked him, 'Where do we buy the ingredients for the sauce?' '*Alimentari*, my dear Watson.' Sherlock's shop has the advantage of selling not only honey, oil, bread, tomato ketchup, butter and cheese, all of which are to be snapped up on the spot, but also rum, vodka and Cointreau, which are vital for the good of the watermelon.

Home immediately. Time to get someone else to make the salad, the dressing, to wrap the potatoes in foil, and to make the sweet and sour sauce. Time for me to make the Bomba and collect some wood. Time for everyone to have a Camp. Sod. Good Lord. Here they come. Where's the wheelbarrow? Pile it all in, escort them to wherever we're going, light the fire, settle them down, give them a drink and have a lovely time.

Spare ribs: on the grill.

Sweet and sour sauce: take tomato ketchup (Heinz is best), squeezed lemons, honey, rosemary, and anything else in the cupboard.

Potatoes: wrap in silver foil and bung on the fire.

Salad and dressing: search me.

Bomba

Slice the very top off a big watermelon. Take out the inside with a spoon and your hands. Squidge the insides through a colander into a pot. For a big melon put one bottle of rum, one of vodka and a little Cointreau into the empty shell of the fruit. Add as much of the juice as will fit in, leaving room for ice. Vary strength as seen fit.

James Lees-Milne

James Lees-Milne came to Holkham once or twice and I was thrilled when one of his diaries was published in which he comments rather nicely on how I looked. He was a friend of Diana Mitford and said to have been a lover of her brother Tom. He was a very well-known architectural historian and expert on country houses. He married Alvide, Viscountess Chaplin, who was a landscape gardener and whilst he is said to have had an affair with Harold Nicholson in the 1930s, she apparently had one with Harold's wife, Vita Sackville-West. James was not a man for typical country estate pursuits, but he and his wife lived in the mid 1970s at Essex House on the Badminton Estate of Master, the Duke of Beaufort who, when Lees-Milne's dog escaped and messed up the hunt, is said to have declared, 'What's the point of the Lees-Milnes? They don't hunt. They don't shoot. What use are they?'

I Loathe Picnics
James Lees-Milne

I loathe picnics.

It may be hereditary. My parents also loathed them as much as they disliked each other, and certainly as much as they disliked us. By some inexplicable mischance it became an established family custom that on the birthday of my sister, my brother and myself, the five of us went in a hired punt and one canoe on the River Avon for a picnic. To make matters worse, we three children were all born in August. So too was my mother, but I think that only one year did we go on four of these ghastly expeditions in this ill-fated month.

We embarked at Evesham and sailed (if that is the right word) in deadly silence either up or downstream. If we started downstream there was the impending horror of having to battle against the current on the way back. If we started upstream there was the weir, which meant dragging or carrying the boats several yards overland and the certainty of one of us losing his or her temper. Now the extraordinary thing was that in those distant days when summers were summers and the sun shone from morn till eve, it always rained on our birthdays, not intermittently, but consistently, heavily and often catastrophically. Of course we knew beforehand that this would be the case. Nonetheless we went because our parents supposed that we children enjoyed the outings, and that they must dutifully subordinate their strong disinclination to our pleasure. It was only when we were grown up that we dared admit how much we had disliked these expeditions. Our parents groaned. 'If only,' my mother said, 'you had told us so when the eldest of you was five.'

In retrospect these countless picnics merge into one because almost invariably they followed the same pattern and the same proceedings repeated themselves. First there was the unloading of basket, rugs, cushions, sunshades, umbrellas, waterproofs and dogs from car to punt and canoe. Next, the embarrassing scene of my father bargaining with the boatman about the charge, which, if I remember rightly, was thirty shillings for the first three hours and five shillings for each subsequent quarter of an hour. This calculation enraged my father who refused to understand why, were we to spend four hours on the river, the last should cost him a whole pound.

'But you might not come back,' the saucy boatman once dared to remonstrate.

'Do you suppose,' my father replied, drawing himself up to his full six foot two and half inches, 'that I would want to go off with your beastly canoe, leaving you with my new Minerva four-seater? Think again, my good man. Besides, don't you know who I am?' Who was he, anyway?

If we started upstream my mother, who insisted upon having the canoe to herself and the dogs, in spite of my father's warnings, invariably got caught in a whirlpool. She would go round and round and round, desperately paddling in one direction, for she could not reverse, until the bull terrier and the Pekineses, made giddy by these gyrations, would jump overboard. This meant that my mother (whose raffia hat had already been knocked off by an overhanging branch) capsized before her madly rotating canoe reached the bank. My father, cursing and swearing 'I told you so', would stretch out the punt pole, exhorting her to grasp it while he towed her ashore. His propulsion of the punt, with the struggling body of his wife at the end of it, was an exceedingly awkward operation for him and an uncomfortable experience for her. At least her immersion settled the vexed question of where to have the picnic. If she hadn't fallen in we would have spent ages looking for the right landing place, the right amount of shade (should a ray of sun come out), and the right amount of protection from the inevitable thunderstorm. As it happened, we were obliged to picnic on the sewage farm, next to the gasometer and just beyond the railway siding.

Before we unloaded the picnic basket and other paraphernalia my mother was obliged to strip to the skin, clean off the stinking mud with tufts of rushes and then be wrapped, shivering, with those rugs on which, had the accident not occurred, we would have sat. Thus she squatted like some Egyptian mummy under an igloo of umbrellas. By now my father was in a filthy temper. He, who was by nature a very practical man, refused to do anything but read the *Morning Post* (always a bad sign) which he was obliged to do standing up. He left us children to unpack the basket and spread the paper plates and food on the soggy ground (every rug and mackintosh enveloping my mother). The smell of sewage, gas and my mother was very unappetising.

Reclining on one elbow with nothing to lean against, even when not eating and drinking with the free hand, has always been torture to me. Besides, the sewage farm did not provide grass, but cinders, if I remember correctly, over which there passed at regular intervals a long, revolving arm which sprayed disinfectant. Memory tells me too that there was seldom enough to eat on our picnics. It never occurred to my mother to tell the cook what food we needed. It was left to the cook to supply chunks of bread and dripping (which children in those days were supposed to like), fids of salty gammon, a few unripe plums and, of course, the birthday cake. On this occasion the bull terrier had sat on the cake, which thereby became a total washout. There would be cider (a great treat) to drink, but not the delicious sweet sort out of a bottle, rather our own home-brewed, bitter sort, unclear and cloudy like some unwholesome liquid from a specimen bottle. There were never enough mugs, and we had to share. I have always had a horror of sharing mugs and would show my disgust. This enraged my father who thought it pathetic. 'Effeminate' was the word he used. Besides, the cider, heady stuff, attracted all the wasps in the Vale of Evesham, as well as little black flies which could not be extracted and had to be swallowed.

After this disgusting and inadequate meal we children had to pack up. We could not take home the remains and my mother – quite rightly – had a horror of litter. We were not allowed to throw the paper in the river, not even the plum stones in case a fish might swallow one and choke. We had to dig a hole with our fingers. Then we had to count the knives, forks and spoons. There was always one missing. From behind the *Morning Post* my father would growl, 'We are not leaving until you have found it.' When it was found my father would put down the paper and yawn. My mother's teeth would chatter. My father would remember an appointment with a man about a horse. He had to get home at once.

We would re-embark. There would be a row among the children about which of us was going to have the canoe because 'shooting the rapids' was the only enjoyable part of the expedition. I, being the most selfish and determined, usually won. Wet, cold, cross and under-nourished, we returned to the boathouse. Looking at his watch, my father would rejoice that we had been on the river for exactly two hours and fifty-five minutes.

How I loathe picnics.

George Christie

A contributor with a similar attitude to picnics as James Lees-Milne was George Christie. I absolutely loved George and his wife Mary, they were great friends. I knew them because George's father John Christie had taught my father at Eton before going on to marry Audrey Mildmay and founding Glyndebourne Opera for her. I used to go and stay with George and Mary at Glyndebourne, first of all in the house and then when their son Gus took over I stayed in a lovely little cottage quite near them. It was all such a pleasure! I've always loved the opera since my grandfather, who was very musical, introduced me to it. I used to dance along to whatever he was playing and frequently went with my father to the operettas, which he adored.

I asked George to write about a picnic because of course Glyndebourne is renowned for the picnics everyone takes to eat in the grounds before the opera, and he agreed. I went to take a photograph of him with my little box brownie and suggested it might be rather fun to take one of him in the ha-ha with the cows behind and picnickers off to the left. Of course he plunged straight into the ha-ha wearing his dinner jacket and I took what

I thought was a rather good photograph! I had imagined he would write about how amazing picnics are at Glyndebourne but, in fact, he writes about how he doesn't like picnics at all and can't understand why people who come to the opera prefer sitting on a rug, which is really very uncomfortable, rather than going into the dining room, which then was quite small but where they could get a very good dinner in comfort.

It's wonderful that George's son Gus Christie has also given us a picnic for this book. Gus inherited Glyndebourne and is married to the brilliant opera singer Danielle de Niese. His picnic gives us a sense of how Glyndebourne has evolved since George's time, and how the passion for picnicking among the audience is undimmed as the provisions and space for it in the gardens have improved.

Glyndebourne: A Critical View of the Picnic
George Christie

Picnics are difficult to stomach. I for one don't have much appetite for them. The human body, it seems to me, is not a suitable shape for eating in comfort at ground level. Eating in this fashion ought to be anti-digestive; so it should follow that the second half of performance at Glyndebourne gets a dyspeptic reception. Less than fifty per cent of the audience can be fed in the restaurant – so something over thirty thousand people picnic in the Glyndebourne gardens each year – a disturbing volume of dyspepsia in my book.

However, the British music critic confounds this theory. He is convinced that the Glyndebourne audience is recklessly receptive to the second part of a performance, having suffered or tolerated the first. Is the Glyndebourne audience a glutton for punishment, as I suspect? Or is the Glyndebourne audience simply a glutton, as the British music critic would like us to believe? Or does the British music critic himself tend to picnic at Glyndebourne and so prove the theory that cynicism is born of dyspepsia? Thirty thousand eating their way through their picnics in the relentless rain of the 1980 summer must surely have tested the audience's resilience. But their frailty remains to be proved. The box office for 1981 was as snowed under as ever. Perhaps the audience comes for the performance rather than the picnic...

In 1976 a device was introduced to make picnics more palatable at Glyndebourne. A large marquee was put up in the grounds, a result of the munificence of W.D. and H.O. Wills. At a ceremony held to celebrate the opening of this marquee, I made a few fatuous remarks about hoping for a wet summer. It turned out to be the hottest, driest summer in recorded history, and the marquee was a wasted asset. Everybody was praying for the rains. The next three summers answered their prayers and swamped the place – so we had to extend the marquee (and, I hope, the receptivity of the audience as well as that of the British music critic).

The picnic ritual at Glyndebourne is relentlessly publicised. Many of the foreign critics devote the first part of their 'appreciation' to a description of the resemblance of the Friesian cattle on one side of the ha-ha to the audience grazing on the other. They invariably devote the next part of their 'appreciation' to a nostalgic, rather than pertinent, walk down Glyndebourne's memory lane; as a token to their profession as critics, they throw in at the end a line or two about the performance which straddles either side of the picnic.

One of the little foibles of Glyndebourne's picnickers is to tie bits of string round the neck of their bottles and moor them to the banks of the ponds to keep the wine cool. One audience member fell in while dragging his bottle out. A resourceful usher showed the luckless man to the wardrobe department, who helped him out with a smart costume from the Bal Blanc scene from the final act of *Eugene Onegin*. The man enjoyed his Blanc de Blanc and turned out to be a critic from California. The enthusiasm of his article was effusive. The temptation to encourage critics to moor their bottles is a strong one, but I suppose it must be resisted!

Gus Christie

My Dad's description of the Glyndebourne picnics is a hard act to follow but I'm delighted to report that our audiences are still as passionate, if not more, about having a picnic in the long interval – thank god, the English are creatures of habit and will often return to their same favoured spot and, I imagine, with the same picnic food each year. When the new theatre was built thirty years ago, there was not much provision for undercover picnickers on wet nights and the foyers around the theatre were crammed with tables and rugs on the brick walkways and it resembled a very glamorous refugee camp. We have now sprouted marquees and stretch tents, so that people can spill out into the gardens on the wet and windy nights as well.

The garden continues to evolve and we have pushed the fence out into the field and created some beautiful new picnicking areas amongst meadows teeming with orchids. One of mine and many people's favourite spots is under the dappled shade of the walnut trees near my mum's abundant rose garden.

You rarely see people spread out on rugs these days and I agree with my dad about the discomfort of ground-level picnicking but nothing beats sitting out on a summer's evening surrounded by others enjoying themselves and our blessed setting.

The local wildlife can be problematic, the canny jackdaws in particular, who now know that the bells summoning the audiences back into the theatre at the end of the interval signals that in about ten minutes the lawns will be clear and it will time to move in for the leftovers. So now we have sporadic crop-scarer bangs and are even imitating the jackdaw alarm calls to keep them at bay, and allow audiences to return, on the balmier nights, for a last drink at dusk.

Josceline Dimbleby

I was so delighted when Josceline said she would write about a picnic for us. She is a wonderful cook, married then to David Dimbleby. I had met her former father-in-law Richard Dimbleby because he was so much a part of the Coronation. He was the pre-eminent voice of the BBC and was doing the commentary for the television broadcast. He either owned or had rented a houseboat which he brought up to be as near to Westminster Abbey as possible and was great fun at the rehearsal. He had a very high vantage point as the abbey was built up on either side of the aisle with rows of seating almost up to the rafters. He teased us maids of honour, saying he was going to be keeping an eye on us all from up there. I remember rather nervously saying to him, 'Well I hope we don't mess it up. I do hope it all goes according to plan!'

Josceline's Devonshire picnic is so evocative and her recipes are of course mouthwatering!

Devonshire Picnic
Josceline Dimbleby

Halfway up to Totnes on the River Dart there is a peninsula of majestic oak and beech trees; it has green sun-dappled banks and we know it as Picnic Point. Almost every day during the school holidays in Devon we picnic. We sail to coves along the coast, or we drive on to Dartmoor for long walks through forests, rewarded by a home-made pasty eaten on the mossy banks of a stream. On wild-weather days we row to the other side of the river by our house, to a disused quarry so sheltered from all winds by its cathedral-like walls that plants grow there of an exotic character quite unexpected in England. But Picnic Point is the most magical place of all. It has a natural fireplace on a promontory looking down into the deep green water, and although there are always signs of others having had a fire there shortly before, we have never, in all our years of Devon life, had to share Picnic Point with anyone.

The boat journey up the Dart is beautiful; most beautiful of all is the calm of early evening in the last yellow sunlight when we often sail up for a picnic supper. One evening we cooked a huge rib of beef – smoky, tender and rare – which we ate by the light of the fire while the children, inspired by the dark woods all round and the river noises, told ghost stories.

Our picnic cooking has been simplified by a large two-sided grill into which the food is clamped and turned over all at once – none of that endless forking of sausages while the smoke chokes and blinds you. We simply put stones on either side of the fire, balance the grill over it, and sit back sipping scrumpy and savouring the smell of the cooking. My children normally profess to dislike sausages, but good butchers' sausages cooked in the smoke of a driftwood fire and stuffed into a fresh bun roll with some mustard and crisp lettuce are always welcome. The other success on the grill is marinaded meat and chicken – the aroma of Indian spices wafting into the English country air has a nice incongruity, and a bold flavour is just what keen outdoor appetites need.

Sometimes when we have set out late we eat on the boat. Tastes are more exciting in the open air, so hot food seems extra special. I often stuff a mixture of grated cheese, onion and herbs, bound with whisked egg, into buttered baps; cook them, wrapped in foil, in a fairly high oven for 15-20 minutes before we leave the house; and wrap the foil up in layers of newspaper. They keep hot for hours, even in the chill of a sea breeze.

Our Devon picnics are an everyday affair. The food is appreciated as much as any I prepare, but the crowded summer days give one no time for elaborate preparation. The special-occasion picnic which I have time to think about, gives me the creative challenge I enjoy best. For Glyndebourne, I once made a game pie decorated musically and inscribed with the words of the opera we were there for, *Così Fan Tutte*. When my children were small we used sometimes to take a large group of their friends for a birthday picnic tea and games in Richmond Park. It gave me great satisfaction to produce an array of brightly coloured cakes, jellies and biscuits set out on the grass on a large white sheet.

Then there are picnics abroad: often uncomfortable, hot, prickly, often not in the perfect spot, but more of a pleasure to shop for. In the East I have had wonderful picnics, prepared in grand, old-fashioned style. I remember one lunch sitting in basket chairs high up above the Ganges at Chunar in central India, eating delicate samosas, spicy meatballs and marinaded chicken out of a basket lined with starched white linen, as we watched and heard a panorama of life on the great river below us.

Having been brought up with all manner of picnics a major part of my life, our nautical Devon feasts have now become most familiar to me, and as a spot which has everything, even its own vegetable crop, the succulent samphire, growing on the mud at low tide, Picnic Point on the River Dart for us reigns supreme.

Grilled Spiced Chicken

(for 6-8)

I find this the most popular picnic food of all. All you have to do is remember to spare a few minutes the night before to prepare the delicious marinade, and in the morning the chicken pieces, tender and aromatic with Indian spices, will be ready to take on your picnic. They will cook well either over charcoal or on a simple grill over a wood fire. If you must, you can cook them in advance on your grill at home – in any case they are excellent cold. You can use any joints of chicken but I find inexpensive chicken wings very successful. Of course, you can vary the spices according to what you have.

1½-2 lb (700-900 g) small chicken joints

For the Marinade

- 1 onion, sliced roughly
- 1-inch (2.5 cm) piece of fresh ginger, peeled and chopped roughly
- 6–8 cloves garlic, peeled
- 3 teaspoons ground coriander
- 2 teaspoons ground cinnamon

2 teaspoons ground cardamom
½ teaspoon chilli powder or cayenne
3 tablespoons red wine vinegar
3 tablespoons sunflower oil
1 tablespoon tomato purée
1 rounded teaspoon salt

Simply put all the marinade ingredients into a liquidiser or food processor and whizz to a smooth paste. Pour the marinade over the chicken joints, stir to coat thoroughly, and leave in a covered bowl in the refrigerator or a cool place overnight.

Grill over a high heat on both sides until almost blackened.

Beef and Onion Flatbreads

(for 5-6)

These are rather like a wholemeal pancake incorporating minced beef and onion. You can wrap them up in foil while they are hot and then in thick newspaper to keep them warm until you reach your picnic place. Alternatively you can eat them cold. Either way, take with you a box of cut lettuce, tomato and fresh mint leaves and wrap the flatbreads round a stuffing of this mixture. They are delicious and nutritious, and children love them too.

1 large onion
4 oz (110 g) minced beef
½–1 teaspoon chilli powder
12 oz (350 g) wholemeal or 85% wholewheat flour
sunflower oil for frying
salt

Peel the onion and chop very finely. Mix with the minced beef in a large bowl. Season with chilli powder and a generous sprinkling of salt. Add the flour and mix in with your hands. Gradually stir in up to 4 pints (150 ml) water – enough to make the mixture stick together. Knead on a well-floured board for 3–4 minutes. Then take egg-sized handfuls of the dough and shape these into round balls. Sprinkle board and rolling pin with flour to prevent sticking, and roll out the dough as thinly as you can. Heat about ¼ inch (5 mm) oil in a large frying pan. Fry the breads one by one at a medium-to-high heat, turning once, until brown on each side. Drain on absorbent paper and pile on a serving dish in a very low oven to keep warm until you are ready to leave.

Arabella Boxer

Another famous cook who contributed a picnic is Arabella Boxer. She was great fun and we all loved being invited to dinner by her and her then husband, the magazine editor and cartoonist Mark Boxer, as you knew you were going to get a very, very good dinner. We all had her cookbooks, *First Slice Your Cookbook* was an absolute bible, we couldn't have a dinner party without using an Arabella Boxer recipe. Not that we were cooking them ourselves, as back then most of us had cooks. (Shamefully I cooked my first meal in my eighties when I found myself living on my own in Norfolk.) The air picnic she wrote for us was brilliant. The food on aeroplanes was always disgusting, and usually rather bad for you, so that years later when my best friend Margaret Vyner and I made our annual trip to India we used to take an Arabella Boxer Air Picnic with us. She was always rather strict about no alcohol, which we found rather harder to stick to, but we did limit ourselves to just one or two glasses of wine and always ended up arriving in fine fettle.

A Picnic for the Air
Arabella Boxer

In the early days of travel, passengers invariably took their food with them. Towards the end of her life, my Scottish grandmother admitted that she had never eaten a meal in public; perhaps she didn't eat when travelling, or perhaps she just didn't travel. For us, living as we did in the north of Scotland, overnight train trips were a part of life; travelling back and forth to school, visits to the dentist and optician – all involved lengthy journeys. One of the nicest things about them was sitting on the top bunk of a third-class sleeper – only our parents travelled first-class – unwrapping the greaseproof paper package of food that was meant to sustain one through the night. Torn between greed and potential travel sickness, I always ended up eating everything, but have felt unable to face the same foods since; sandwiches made with roast beef or chicken still make me feel slightly faint.

On the Trans-Siberian Express, travellers took their own uncooked food with them; the train had a special 'cold' carriage for storing semi-frozen food. Passengers would take with them a large bag of *pelmeni*, a sort of Russian ravioli, and at each station a large pot of water was kept boiling over a brazier, so that the *pelmeni* could be cooked while the train stopped. In England we were not so lucky, and all food had to be prepared in advance and packed.

Few people take packed meals on trains any more, although it would be sensible to do so. There is something slightly daunting about eating alone, surrounded by strangers who are not eating, and trips to the dining car – if there is such a thing – are fun, though expensive and gastronomically disappointing. If, however, one is travelling by air, there is a very strong case for taking one's own food, and one's own drink as well. In the early days of Laker flights this was essential, for food was not provided, and it seemed an eminently sensible economy. From the passenger's point of view, taking one's own food on any regular airline is not of course an economy, since meals are provided free, but rather a sensible form of insurance. This is especially true, paradoxically, when travelling first-class, for the food and drink that are then pressed on us are even less suited to our needs than the ordinary fare. In fact, I have recently discovered that most airlines will provide special vegetarian meals if they are ordered a day or two in advance. Being lower in protein, and more easily digested, they provide a reasonable alternative for occasions when preparing a 'home-cooked' meal is impractical.

When flying, our system is under strain from a number of different factors. The most obvious one is pressure: although the aircraft is pressurised, for technical reasons it cannot be brought down to the pressure that most of us are accustomed to – sea level. Instead, it is kept at the pressure found between six and seven thousand feet – within moments of entering the plane our bodies have to adjust to a significant change in environment. Pressurisation causes the gases in our system to dilate, creating an unpleasant feeling of distention. For this reason it is important not to drink fizzy liquids.

The second main reason for feeling less than well is the dehydration of the air in the cabin. This puts the kidneys under strain since it is their job to regulate the balance of water in the blood. When we are in danger of becoming dehydrated, the pituitary gland produces large amounts of anti-diuretic hormone, causing the kidneys to re-absorb into the bloodstream much of the water which would have been excreted. In order to offset this dehydration, it is vital to drink a great deal; for short journeys, roughly one pint for every hour spent in the air is advisable, while for long trips a quarter of a pint per hour is more realistic. Still mineral water or hot herb teas are ideal.

Alcohol should be avoided at all costs. First it exacerbates dehydration, and secondly it causes extra work for the liver, which is already operating under strain. The liver is responsible for breaking down and getting rid of poisons absorbed into the body, for example those contained in alcohol, caffeine and nicotine. When travelling, the liver is already under pressure and less able than usual to cope with these tasks, so that drinking alcohol and coffee and smoking should be avoided. The liver also controls the degree of acidity in the body, so that very acid foods such as citrus fruits should be kept to a minimum. Champagne is a good example of what to avoid, since it combines three of the worst things: alcohol, acidity and gas.

In addition to the strains caused by pressurisation, dehydration, altitude and speed other stresses are normally connected with travel: fatigue, anxiety and, in many cases, fear of flying itself. All these affect the nervous system, which in turn affects the digestion, therefore foods that put an undue strain on the digestive organs should be avoided. Rich foods, due to their high fat content, come into this category, as do foods that are high in protein. Meat, eggs and cheese should only be eaten in very small quantities, while indigestible foods like hard-boiled eggs and cold potatoes (i.e. potato salad) are also best left out. Highly spiced food like salami is also unsuitable, while garlic is clearly antisocial, to say the least.

A good general rule is to drink as much as possible, remembering to stick to still, non-alcoholic drinks, and to eat as little as possible. The food should be similar to that given to a convalescent: bland, light, easy to digest and appetising. It should be moderate in temperature, neither iced nor boiling hot. Creamy vegetable soups, so long as they are not too rich, salads, small pieces of chicken or white fish, cooked vegetables (except potatoes), rice, fruit, yoghurt and low-fat cream cheese are all good. Still mineral water should be carried in generous quantities; it is no good relying on the stewardess to bring you water, for she will be too busy, and the glasses are minute. Mineral water, especially a still one, is rarely among the drinks on offer. (A 'bottle' bag for carrying a large bottle of mineral water can always be used later to carry off duty-free drink bought on the plane.) Teabags of herb tea are useful, since these are easily diluted with hot water when the stewardess does the coffee.

Planning a picnic to take from home is relatively simple, but finding a suitable meal to bring back, without a base to prepare it, is another matter. Yet most other countries are better equipped for this sort of thing than we are, and a brief visit to a delicatessen just before leaving will usually provide mineral water, vegetable juice (for a soup substitute), bread, butter, fruit, yoghurt and a low-fat cheese such as fromage blanc or ricotta.

It is both sensible and fun to shop around to build up a small picnic kit. A light basket with a lid, or a small cool bag, equipped with plastic plate and beaker, two plastic containers with lids, plus knife, fork and spoon, should cover every eventuality. Those who abhor plastic can find old horn beakers, reminiscent of shooting parties, in antique shops, while a wooden plate can replace the plastic one, although it will be heavier. Once the habit has become established, it takes little time to prepare a couple of simple dishes before leaving, and the benefit in avoiding, or at least decreasing, the after-effects of air travel will certainly repay the extra effort.

Menus for Air Picnics

1. Creamy leek soup
   Potted shrimps
   Brown bread and butter sandwich
   Yoghurt
2. Cold cucumber soup with dill
   Breast of poached chicken wrapped in a lettuce leaf
   Watercress salad
   Crême caramel, baked in an *oeuf en cocotte* dish
3. Prawn and crisp lettuce salad
   Sandwich of brown bread and butter and cress, or watercress
   Petits Suisses
4. Beef tea
   Chicken salad
   Matzos or Ryvita
   Grated apple in yoghurt
5. Chicken broth (in thermos)
   Salad of cooked vegetables
   Plums, grapes or cherries
6. Flaked white fish in mayonnaise-type dressing
   Watercress salad
   Brown bread and butter
   Low-fat cream cheese
7. Creamy potato and chervil soup (cold)
   Spinach and mozzarella salad
   Apricots with yoghurt

To drink:
Volvic or other still mineral water
Peppermint, verbena or sage tea

Margaret Vyner

Margaret Vyner is my best friend, I've known her all my life. She was a model who may have walked for the shows but was mainly a photographic model and an artist. I can hardly remember how we met but it was probably at one of the endless weekend parties or dinners we used to go to at that time. Margaret and her husband Henry had a lovely house in Yorkshire, Fountains Hall, near Fountain's Abbey, but we also used to live near them in London. She's my travelling companion, it can be quite hard travelling with people but it was wonderful that we both found someone we could travel with. We want to do the same things and always share a room in hotels; we are very polite around each other, trying not to bang about or turn the light on suddenly in the middle of the night. We've been to India twenty-six times together, travelling all over the country, always chatting away, together with our friend Mitch Crites, the three of us have enjoyed endless picnics together in India.

Dominican Picnic
Margaret Vyner

Dominica, lying between Martinique and Guadeloupe, unloved by many tourists for its black beaches and incessant rain, brought back childhood memories of my grandfather's Victorian conservatory with the smell of damp and warmth and faintly rotting vegetation. The hotel where we stayed was deep in the hilly rain forest. When we arrived it was nearly empty but we were intrigued to find on a noticeboard a mysterious small card advertising 'DOMINICA SAFARIS', which promised a drive round the island followed by a picnic beside a river where we could swim; so, not knowing what to expect, we booked in.

On the appointed morning a brand-new sand-coloured Range Rover appeared, driven by a handsome, bearded West Indian in a matching sand-coloured safari suit and an Ernest Hemingway hat; as we set off we felt that had it been cold he would have tucked a rug round our knees.

The drive itself was breathtaking: in spite of the word safari, we saw nothing but vegetation of such enormity and density that at any moment a Douanier Rousseau tiger might have appeared. We arrived eventually on the site of our picnic: huge rocks, huge ferns and a fast-flowing icy-cold clear river and not a soul in sight. Our driver said that while we swam he would lay out the picnic. When we emerged, starving and half expecting sandwiches and bananas, we were astonished by what we saw. Spread out on a white damask cloth straight from an Edwardian shooting party was the most ravishing and delicious feast imaginable.

First of all, we were given ice-cold rum punches in crystal glasses, and while we sat on the rocks drinking them we gazed greedily at what was to come: stuffed crabs, exotic chicken, avocado mousse, sweet potato bread and mango ice cream. Euphoric after our rum punches (particularly delicious as the Dominican rum and limes are famously good) we set to, and it all tasted as wonderful as it looked, especially as the driver produced a bottle of Clos des Mouches tasting of primroses. Like all good picnics, it seemed to go on for hours, and the experience of enjoying wonderful food and drink in a jungle setting – ferns, plantains, the warm damp air and the only sound (apart from sighs of gluttonous pleasure) that of the running river – was unforgettable.

Two years later we came back to Dominica longing to repeat the experience, but we looked in vain for the card at the hotel, asked in vain about Dominica Safaris, and were met with blank faces – it seemed not so much to have vanished without trace as never to have existed: it had been a *Marie Celeste* of picnics.

Stuffed Crabs

Land crabs are used on the island for this first-course dish.

> 6 small hard-shell crabs
> 3 oz (75 g) freshly made breadcrumbs
> 1 fresh hot pepper, seeded and chopped fine, or hot pepper sauce to taste
> 3 tablespoons chopped chives
> 2 tablespoons chopped parsley
> 2 cloves garlic, crushed
> 1 tablespoon fresh lime juice
> salt and freshly ground pepper
> ¼ teaspoon allspice

3 tablespoons Madeira or dark rum, preferably
    Martinique or Guadeloupe *rhum vieux*
butter

Preheat the oven to gas mark 4 (350°F, 180°C). Plunge the crabs into boiling water and boil for 8–10 minutes. Remove and cool. Take out the meat from the shells and claws and chop it finely. Discard the spongy fibre. Scrub out the empty shells, if small, and reserve. Mash 2 oz (50 g) of breadcrumbs into the crabmeat until the mixture is quite smooth. Add the hot pepper, chives, parsley, lime juice, salt, pepper, allspice, Madeira or rum, mixing thoroughly. Stuff the reserved crab shells with the mixture. If using three or four larger crabs, use the meat to stuff six scallop shells or put in ramekins. Sprinkle with the remaining breadcrumbs and dot with butter. Bake for 30 minutes, or until lightly browned.

If live crabs are not available, buy 1 lb (450 g) of fresh, frozen or tinned crabmeat, or buy plain boiled crabs.

Chicken Calypso

(serves six)

5 tablespoons olive oil
4 lb (1 kg 800 g) chicken, cut into serving pieces
1 lb 2 oz (500 g) rice
1 medium onion, finely chopped
1 clove garlic, chopped
1 green bell pepper, seeded and chopped
1 small hot green pepper, seeded and chopped
8 oz (225 g) mushrooms, sliced

½ teaspoon saffron
piece of lime peel
1 tablespoon lime juice
¼ teaspoon Angostura bitters
2 pints (1 litre 140 ml) chicken stock
salt and freshly ground pepper
3 tablespoons light rum

Heat 3 tablespoons of the oil in a skillet and sauté the chicken pieces until brown all over. Remove to a heavy casserole. Add the rice, onion, garlic, bell pepper and hot pepper to the oil remaining in the skillet and sauté, stirring until the oil is absorbed, being careful not to let the rice scorch. Add to the chicken in the casserole. Add the remaining 2 tablespoons of oil to the skillet, and sauté the mushrooms over a fairly high heat for 5 minutes. Add to the casserole with the saffron, lime peel, lime juice, bitters, stock and salt and pepper to taste. Cover and simmer gently until the rice and chicken are tender and the liquid absorbed – about 30 minutes. Add the rum and cook uncovered for 5 minutes longer.

Hartley Augiste's Rum Punch

(serves one)

2 fl. oz (55 ml) Dominica rum or light rum from
   Martinique or Guadeloupe
½ fl. oz (15 ml) lime juice
3 teaspoons simple syrup (see below)
2–3 dashes Angostura bitters
3–4 ice cubes
maraschino cherry

Combine ingredients in a cocktail shaker and shake hard. Strain over ice cubes.

Simple Syrup

>   1 lb (450 g) granulated sugar
>   ¾ pint (425 ml) cold water

Combine the two in a bowl and stir from time to time until dissolved. Use in drinks instead of sugar. 1 tablespoon of syrup = 1½ teaspoons of sugar

Mango Ice Cream

>   4 eggs
>   4 oz (110 g) sugar
>   ¾ pint (425 ml) milk
>   1 cup of mango pulp mixed with 2 oz (50 g) sugar
>   (extra to above)
>   ½ teaspoon vanilla essence

Beat the eggs lightly with the sugar. Scald the milk and stir into the eggs. Cook the egg mixture on top of a double boiler over hot water, stirring constantly until the mixture coats the spoon. Cool and add mango pulp. Freeze to a mush. Remove from the refrigerator and beat well. Freeze again.

Mitch Crites

It was Colin who first met Mitch Crites when he was building houses on Mustique. On the suggestion of Princess Margaret, Colin had asked the theatre designer Oliver Messel to design all the houses on the island. For his own house Colin wanted to create a Taj Mahal-like home and brought in Mitch Crites, an American living in India who dealt in Indian arts and crafts, to advise him and buy Indian furniture and artefacts to furnish the house. Colin invited Mitch to his 60th birthday Peacock Ball on the island, which is when I met him. I'd been to India once on a trip organised by a magazine with a friend – it had been the most extraordinary holiday with elephants, fireworks and spectacular parties, I absolutely loved it, and had gone mad buying all sorts of unsuitable things which we brought back. Mitch said that if we wanted to go back to India he would look after us. I jumped at the offer, and Margaret and I went to stay with him. We accompanied him on his trips around the country, seeing parts of India we would never otherwise have seen and staying in some pretty rough places, but that didn't matter, we had a brilliant time and Mitch made it all such fun. He is a fluent

Hindi speaker, which made all the difference to how we were received and what we could do. The trip became an annual event and we would return with all sorts of lovely things, saris, scarves, different pieces each year and hold an exhibition in his showroom behind Christie's. Princess Margaret used to come and we'd sell our wares, which people would buy for Christmas presents, we got quite a reputation. Mitch is a very dear friend and I do hope that I will manage one more trip to India, to visit him.

Picnics in India
Mitch Crites

Lady Anne, Margaret Vyner and I bonded at the grand 60th birthday party that Colin, Lord Glenconner and Anne's husband, threw for himself and a shipload full of friends, movie stars and exotic guests on the Caribbean island of Mustique in 1986.

I had been based in India since the late sixties and it was only natural to invite 'Les Girls', as I called Anne and Margaret, to visit my wife, Nilou and me in Delhi and Jaipur, and to tour some of the legendary sites. Over the years, we travelled the length and breadth of India in fourteen fascinating excursions. The one rule that they both insisted on was that Colin was not allowed to join us. But, of course, he did come on his own, shopping for his mansions, restaurants and architectural follies that he loved creating on Mustique and St Lucia. Unlike Les Girls, he could be hard to handle.

I remember once Colin told me that he wanted to buy baskets of costume jewellery for a party he was planning. We took a local tuk-tuk deep into the heart of the 17th-century bazaar in Old Delhi and Colin began selecting glittering bangles and baubles, necklaces and earrings from the local street vendors.

He had told me in advance not to call him by his title but the minute we arrived he loudly announced that he was Lord Glenconner and, instantly, it seemed that we had been transported back to the days of the British Raj. After an hour of haggling, Colin asked for the bill and proclaimed that he wanted to pay by credit card and, naturally, the trolley owner replied that he only took cash. Colin went ballistic and threw the bags of jewellery back in his face. Suddenly, a hostile angry crowd surrounded us. I, somehow, managed to hand over a wad of rupees to the guy for his trouble and we leapt into our waiting scooter and sped off. We were lucky to have escaped unharmed. Colin thought it was jolly good fun and I was left exhausted and a bit shaken.

Anne and Margaret loved being on the road with Meva Singh, our loyal Rajput driver. I would map out a two- to three-week tour in some remote part of the country and we would set off. I sat with Meva in the front watching the road while Anne and Margaret were in the back happily chatting away. The highlight of each day was the ritual picnic. We would often drive for kilometres searching for the perfect site, which had to have shade, a stream or pond, a monument, if possible, and, of course, a nearby 'mustard field' as it came to be called, where they could disappear into the vegetables or tall grass for a moment of privacy.

The picnic menu didn't vary much as it suited the warm and humid weather and we all liked it. It included vegetable cutlets, cheese sandwiches on white bread, boiled eggs, sliced tomatoes, red carrots and cucumbers, ketchup packets and seasoning, mango pickle, local sweets and whatever fresh fruit we could find. Also, mineral water and flasks of boiling water for tea.

After lunch, we would relax a while and then continue the journey. Anne and Margaret were wonderful travelling companions. They never complained and were always up for an adventure. As soon as we arrived in the late afternoon at an old palace converted into a hotel or a jungle bungalow, I would ask the maharaja or local guides what's happening in the area. Are there any obscure monuments, local markets or tribal festivals going on? No matter how difficult and bumpy the road was to get to an 'event', they were always ready. We explored village stepwells, palaces and soaring forts and laughed together from morning to evening. These are precious memories that I cherish until today.

Rupert Loewenstein

Rupert was the Rolling Stone's financial manager and he and his wife Josephine were some of our closest friends. They were very brave coming out to Mustique in the early days when there was no running water or electricity but they fell in love with it, eventually buying a house there. Rupert was part of a group, along with Jonathan Guinness, who bought a merchant bank in the 1960s, not long after which he was introduced to Mick Jagger and has been credited with transforming the Stones into a global brand. He was responsible for introducing Mick Jagger to Mustique, who also became a friend after coming to the golden ball Colin threw one year. Bianca Jagger came looking absolutely wonderful in a gold crinoline dress and Mick looked rather weird in a little straw pixie hat sprayed gold. But Mick fell in love with the island and has been the most wonderful asset to Mustique – he helped finance a new school and played cricket with the villagers. I think his children almost think of it as home. We used to have wonderful Christmases there when he was with Jerry Hall, playing games and indulging in amateur theatricals. One year we let it be known that we were putting on a play in which

Mick was playing the doctor and Rupert his assistant and were in need of people to play his patients. There was a queue halfway round the island desperate to be examined by Mick, with my nanny Barbara at the front of it!

Rupert, who was a Bavarian prince, was also responsible for introducing Princess Margaret to some of her German relatives on Prince Philip's side. Initially she was rather reluctant, but Rupert persuaded her to go and they ended up visiting Germany several times to stay with various friends and relations which she loved. Princess Margaret had a coterie of gentlemen, among whom were Rupert and Colin, who at Christmas used to take her somewhere lovely for lunch, preferably near Bond Street. They would suggest they might take a stroll afterwards whereupon they would vie with each other as to who had bought her the most expensive present in Cartier or Tiffany's.

'Caldo e Cremoso'
Rupert Loewenstein

Although, like many spoilt men, I prefer the pleasures of the table in the great indoors, there can be exceptions. The pleasures of the table embrace not only what is to be eaten and drunk, but also the civilised enjoyment of good company in an attractive and comfortable setting. Increasingly I have found that wit flourishes in an atmosphere of good food and drink. Perhaps that is because I have never known (and indeed, do they still exist?) the salons where brilliant conversation is enjoyed, while the guests are only fortified by warm lemonade and, perhaps, a plate of 'fingers'.

In a happier age, in the days of good King Idris, we stayed with Italian friends in Tripoli. The day after we arrived we were taken in a bus to look at the ruins of Sabratha, some sixty or seventy miles away across the desert. Having admired the antique splendours for an hour or two in the scorching sun, our hostess asked us whether we were ready for luncheon. Thereupon we rounded a corner and saw set up in front of the huge pillars looking on to the sea a table covered with gleaming linen and, behind comfortable chairs, two footmen in neat white coats with appropriately armorial buttons.

What did we eat and drink? Cool white wine from Maser, hot cannelloni, *vitello tonnato*, some cheese with North African bread, and grapefruit sorbet. The unexpectedness in the desert of this luxury, which originally we had taken to be a mirage, and the pleasure of the company of great friends in beautiful surroundings, was such as to make it one of the most enjoyable luncheons I have ever had.

When we complimented our hostess on the delights of the day, she said, 'Always remember, for a picnic some of the food must be "caldo e cremoso".'

Bryan Adams

Bryan became a close friend after he bought one of the original houses on Mustique. He was very close to Colin, which is rather strange because they were so different. Bryan is a vegan and very controlled, immensely hard working and Colin was quite the opposite, but Bryan understood him. When Colin died on St Lucia, Bryan went to the trouble of hiring a plane to come to the funeral with one or two friends. He'd written a song, 'You're My Friend', which he sang in the church at the huge funeral we had where hundreds of local people had a picture of Colin stuck to their shirts and were waving black balloons. Bryan's father was in the army and, like me, he is very punctual. I saw him the last time I was on Mustique and he arranged to pick me up for lunch at six minutes to one, assuming I'm sure, I would be late, but there I was ready to go at six minutes to one, and he got out of his car and saluted me. I had to tell him it was thirty-four years of training as lady-in-waiting!

On the Road Houmous
Bryan Adams

The perfect recipe on the road.

This is my recipe for something to munch on when in the car travelling from town to town. I usually have something to snack on whilst sitting for hours in the back of a car, so I'll pack some of this, some crudités or carrot and peppers, and naturally some sort of crispy flatbread to accompany it.

A napkin is always useful when hitting a bump.

- 1 can chickpeas
- 4 tablespoons tahini
- 1 whole lemon
- olive oil
- sea salt
- 12 cubes of ice

Drain and rinse the chickpeas and put in food processor with a jar of tahini (to taste) plus the juice of 1 lemon and a big glug of olive oil. Blend on full speed for about 3 minutes until it becomes a smooth paste. Once the mixture is smooth, add ice and continue to blend. The houmous will go pale and creamy. Store in airtight Kilner jar in fridge until needed and serve with basket of flatbread and/or sliced carrots and peppers.

Mary Hayley Bell

We met Mary and her husband, the actor John Mills, when we were accompanying Princess Margaret to a film premiere. Mary was a writer and an actor who wrote *Whistle Down the Wind* starring their daughter Hayley Mills. When I was made Lady-in-Waiting I think Colin rather thought he'd be coming along to everything too and I had to tell him that was not how it worked, although he did sometimes come with us to evening events. On this occasion he came with us to the premiere and when chatting to Mary and John, Colin told them all about Mustique and invited them to come and visit. We had a lovely time with them on the island and I vividly remember one picnic that Colin had arranged where we were all transferred by buggy to Pasture Bay, which was at the end of the island near Princess Margaret's house. The West Indian grape trees up there had all been sculpted by the wind and made the most marvellous sight framing the route down to the beach where Colin had set up a table under the trees. We had a lovely long lunch and then all went swimming together. We really got to know them quite well. I wrote to Mary to tell her about the picnic book and ask if she might contribute to it and she immediately said yes and sent hers very quickly. She was born in Shanghai where her father was serving in the Chinese Maritime Customs Service, so it wasn't a surprise that her picnic was one from her childhood enjoyed in China.

Picnic in China
Mary Hayley Bell

The earliest picnics I remember were in China before the Second World War. To us children they were something very special. My grandmother used to tell of picnics in Shanghai, with as many as twelve helpers, and guests riding on ponies to the beautiful canal by their house, Unkaza, where a vast curry was served with chutneys, poppadoms, shrimps and coconuts, not to mention sweets and coffee.

We had wonderful picnics during our childhood in Macao, where my father was Commissioner of Chinese Customs. He had two small armed launches in order to combat smuggling and gunrunning. We used to go aboard preceded by the dining-room and kitchen staff who carried the food in large canisters, and crates of beer and wine. There would probably be about twenty guests. The anchor would be hauled up, and we would set out for Bias Bay, near Hong Kong. The lunch would probably consist of Chinese food: egg flower soup, deep-fried walnut chicken, paper-wrapped beef with shredded cabbage, fresh shrimp and lobster sauce, fried and boiled rice, crabmeat, glazed apples and pancakes. Everyone ate with chopsticks – in fact, my earliest memories of food are of eating with chopsticks.

Before 'Tiffin', as it was called in the East, we would have a swim from the *Pak Tow* or *Lung Tsing* – whichever launch we were in – while the Chinese crew stood by the machine guns watching for pirates – for pirates there were. After half an hour's siesta we would be rowed ashore to the white gleaming beach of Leper Island, with the mountains behind and a distant view of Hong Kong.

Egg Flower Soup

>2 pints (1 litre 150 ml) bone stock
>2 eggs
>vegetable oil
>2 spring onions, chopped
>1 teaspoon salt
>2 tablespoons soya sauce
>½ teaspoon Ve Tsin (optional)
>1 teaspoon vinegar
>pepper

Bring the stock to the boil and remove from the heat. Beat the eggs, mix with a little oil, and pour slowly into the stock. Add the chopped onions and salt and bring to the boil again. Add soya sauce, Ve Tsin (if using), vinegar and pepper. Stir with a ladle and it is ready to serve. The beaten eggs separate into hundreds of little threads on contact with the hot stock, which gives the soup its name.

Crabmeat in Steamed Eggs

>1 large crab
>2 eggs
>1 teaspoon salt

- 1 tablespoon soya sauce
- 2 spring onions, chopped
- 2 tablespoons sherry
- 1 tablespoon lard

Wash the crab and steam for 15 minutes. Remove the meat from the shell. Beat the eggs and mix them with the salt, soya sauce and chopped spring onions. Add the crabmeat, sherry and half a cup of water. Mix thoroughly and add lard. Steam for 20 minutes. It should be the consistency of thick cream. Put in a large thermos and serve with plain rice.

Hugo Vickers

Hugo and I spent hours swimming in the sea together in Mustique where we met at the house of a mutual friend. I'd just been approached about writing *Lady in Waiting* and was really thinking it was beyond me; I didn't see how I could do it and Hugo gave me great confidence to carry on. He was so kind and encouraging. I'd always loved his books. *The Kiss*, which he wrote in 1996 is the most charming book about two sisters in Windsor who he knew and the impact on their lives of one kiss by a man called Dick. I absolutely loved it. So I was thrilled to meet him and now consider him to be a dear friend.

Garter Day Picnic
Hugo Vickers

My favourite annual picnic is Garter Day, the Monday of Ascot week, when the Knights and Ladies and members of the Royal Family process from the state apartments in Windsor Castle to the service in St George's Chapel, their blue velvet robes and bonnets of ostrich plumes swaying gently in the summer breeze. I have now attended fifty-seven of these, starting very young in 1965. My enthusiasm for the day remains undiminished. It never loses its magic. I am on duty in the chapel as Captain of the Lay Stewards.

My day invariably begins in London as I prepare the picnic. Given that I and my guest(s) are smartly dressed, it is important to avoid things that will explode in the hands and stain our clothes. I tend to go for smoked salmon sandwiches, which have minimal bread but a huge and luscious mouthful of smoked salmon in the centre, roughly four slices – with, of course, butter on the bread, a certain amount of lemon and just a dash of pepper. These are nourishing, easy to eat, perfect. Wine or fruit juice according to taste and some chocolate to round it off, all very simple – and it travels in the Diamond Jubilee picnic basket from the pop concert in the gardens of Buckingham Palace in 2012. Driving up the Long Walk towards the castle is special. That is where we eat it. Sometimes we go into the castle's private grounds via Shaw Farm Gate and eat the picnic next to the Sports Ground. In both cases the castle is very much in view.

Between 1980 and 1990 I had a good deal with one of my fellow Lay Stewards from St George's Chapel – Captain Andrew Yates, an elderly naval captain who lived in Old Windsor. He was a founder member of Glyndebourne, and after his wife died, made an annual plan with me. He took four tickets for the opera. I did the driving, brought a guest and prepared the picnic. Andrew insisted on eating it from the boot of the car, which was a bit depressing. He did not want the hassle of carrying it to the lawn. But for his 90th birthday, I surprised him by getting someone to come down and set up an elegant table, as for a dinner party. He loved that. It was also his last Glyndebourne.

Picnics can be fun or they can be a nightmare. Finding yourself in a field with cows or worse still, an angry bull, is not to be recommended — so a bit of reconnaissance is essential. I have a phobia of wasps and they sometimes like to join in a picnic, sending me scurrying. The worst scenario — you swallow one. But if all goes well, there is nothing finer than a picnic on a perfect English summer day, a bottle of wine and a siesta afterwards.

Banana Pudding

Not sure how suitable for a picnic — but my aunt's banana pudding has many enthusiastic followers.

Slice up a quantity of bananas as thin as you can be bothered. In a bowl, crumble up a quantity of Cadbury's milk flake chocolate. Put about two pots of double cream into another bowl, feed in the bananas and the chocolate pieces, and stir them well together. You can add a (considerable) dash of rum if you like. Then just put it into the refrigerator for a few hours till it sets solid. Bring it out, sprinkle some more milk flake pieces on the top to cover it. Delicious.

Colin Tennant

Colin was a brilliant organiser of picnics. Once at Glen he arranged a picnic at the Loch and because his eccentric uncle, Stephen Tennant, thought the colour of heather vulgar, he bought and stuck hundreds of blue paper flowers on the hill. Stephen just said, 'So much better darling boy.'

Mustique
Colin Tennant

A picnic is different. In a cupboard, on a hillside, up a gum tree, down among the dead men – anything out of the daily grind. Herein lies our first problem. In Mustique we have a picnic every day. Second problem, always the same people; and third, always the same food. That's not to say we don't enjoy ourselves. It's like laughing at an old joke. It gets better every time. So here goes, everyone, wait for it!

We meet at the beach.

Lagoon or Macaroni (that's the name of the beach, not the

main course)? Macaroni has waves, and no sandflies. For those that can't handle the ocean, Lagoon has sandflies and no waves. For those that can't handle the sandflies, there's 'off'!

Cold cuts, or chicken? The Great General Store in Mustique rarely sells a whole chicken. More usually on offer are what are termed 'chicken parts'. These are fairer than a regular chicken, because each frozen box contains a number of similar parts, i.e. all legs or all wings. There is no question of having to carve or ask guests, 'Which part would you like?' and being left oneself with a bit of brown. NB Avoid at all costs 'chicken backs'.

A guest. Plenty of choice here. However, remember to tell your guests if the picnic is for somebody's birthday, or alternatively in fancy dress.

A glance in the fridge will tell you all you need to know about cold cuts. The chicken parts are more complicated as they need defrosting and should be grilled or devilled.

Mustique Mule

> 1 fresh coconut (or waternut) per person
> vodka
> lime syrup

Cut off the top of the nut with a cutlass. Pour out some of the milk, pour in vodka, lime syrup and ice cubes. Drink through a straw.

Caution: coconut milk will stain your clothes, irremediably.

Seaweed Supper

For an evening picnic on the beach, wrap whatever fresh fish is available in layers of wet seaweed and grill gently over a fire. When cooked, remove the seaweed and sprinkle with fresh lime juice.

Anne's Ginger Whisky Creams or Pudding

- 1 tablespoon whisky
- 2 tablespoons syrup from stem ginger
- ½ teaspoon powdered ginger
- 2 tablespoons caster sugar
- ½ pint (275 ml) double cream
- 2 egg whites
- 3 pieces of stem ginger to decorate

Place the whisky, ginger syrup, powdered ginger, caster sugar and cream in a bowl and whisk with an egg beater until thick. In another bowl whisk the egg whites until stiff. Fold the egg whites into the ginger mixture, spoon into individual dishes and chill. Decorate with small pieces of chopped stem ginger. Cover with foil and pack into an insulated bag ready for the picnic.

Drue Heinz

When Princess Margaret came to Mustique she always refused to fly back overnight, saying she was far too exhausted. She'd say, 'I think I'll go to America and stay with Drue and then fly back from there,' which is what we always did. Drue was married to Jack Heinz who was heir to the Heinz fortune and exceedingly rich. They had a wonderful house on the Upper East Side in New York and we would go and stay there with her. Drue would throw great parties and dinners for Princess Margaret and there would be endless shopping trips. Princess Margaret loved the shop at the Metropolitan Museum which sold jewellery they had copied from paintings in the collection and which everyone loved. There was a pair of earrings, one white and one black pearl earring which many of us had from there, including Princess Diana. Caroline Herrera was a great friend and used to give Princess Margaret lots of her clothes when we were there. I was allowed to choose one outfit from the ready-to-wear collection, which was amazing.

Drue was always such a kind and generous hostess. She also had a house near Ascot and I remember one party there when she imported a complete fairground into the garden so we could all ride on the dodgems and big swings.

Princess Margaret always invited Drue to her annual visit to the Chelsea Flower show. Each member of the royal family used to take a small party of friends on the Monday afternoon, before the crowds were there. It was one of the treats Princess Margaret used to arrange for us and we'd pretty much have the whole place to ourselves. There was a big tent with tea and drinks and lots of different royal households would go, each household having their own table.

Drue was also a great patron of literature and established various literary retreats. She bought Hawthornden Castle outside Edinburgh and if a writer had had at least one book published they could go along and stay. Lunch would be provided in a hamper outside their room and then in the evening she would throw a huge dinner with all these very interesting people to discuss literature and ideas, you might find yourself sitting next to luminaries like Harold Pinter or Lady Antonia Fraser. She also co-founded a literary press, Ecco Press and the Drue Heinz Literary prize. She had a real sense of fun though, which you can tell from her clambake picnic which I think is so well described.

A New England Clambake
Drue Heinz

By far the messiest of all picnics is the famous American institution called the clambake or, before the price of lobster flew too high out of the water, the lobsterbake. In the twenties and thirties it was entirely different, and even grand. The famous

Marshall Field, for instance, would anchor his great yacht off a beautiful stretch of beach in Maine and instruct his crew to go to it. This meant prepare a clambake for the next evening at sundown for his twenty guests.

Nowadays it is every man for himself. However, the menu has not really changed since the Republic was formed, nor has the way settlers learned to cook the corn and shellfish in the ad hoc ovens, or pits, invented by the Indians. The New England or Yankee clambake is as much a national feast as is Thanksgiving. And most people have a last glorious binge on the beach at the end of August before they return to the city from their long summer holidays.

The first clambake I attended was in Martha's Vineyard on a lovely beach of dunes capped with long willowy beachgrass. I was told to bring a sweater, although the temperature at 5 o'clock was about 85 degrees. I was given a basket to carry, surprisingly heavy. I found out later that it was full of vodka and gin. We arrived to find a blazing fire and much consternation. It was supposed to have turned to embers by then, but the wind had risen and whipped up the blaze. And the smoke – Oh Lord – had everyone coughing, rubbing their eyes, retreating frantically from the 'bake' pits and yelling for drinks.

Soon we were consoled with large gins in paper cups, and someone kept running the line of teary-eyed spectators offering ice, ice, anyone? And along came a teenager shaking peanuts out of a large bag. Unfortunately, most of them fell to the sand as we swayed in the wind, which was becoming stronger and colder. Meanwhile the younger, more durable element had managed to damp down the fire and were endeavouring to place the clams around the blistery seaweed whose water would cook them.

Hours passed, the moon came up, and the wind changed. We had to turn our backs to the fire and wrap our much-needed sweaters around us, at the same time trying to keep the sand from getting into every nook and cranny of our weather-whipped bodies.

But then came the cry, 'Clams up!' Several young men appeared with plates piled with clams, sweet potatoes, corn, a small lobster, and a large paper napkin. My nearest companion turned to grab a plateful when a gust of wind caught us and everything fell into the sand. 'Don't touch it yet, it's burning hot,' went down the line. So we all had another restorative drink.

Eventually we found a bit of everything, gratiné with sand. What to do? Obviously stagger to the sea, wash the sand off the food quickly in the water, and eat it with our fingers. I tried, goodness knows, I tried! But I remember only getting wet to the thighs as a big wave struck, knocking the plate from my hand. Thank heavens it was dark. As I trudged back, jeans clinging dankly to my thighs, someone said, 'What wonderful clams. Didn't you think the lobster was great?' I replied, 'Yes, absolutely wonderful, never had anything so good, but it sure makes one thirsty.'

At least I had managed to hold on to my cup and received an immediate fill-up. As I neared the fire, I managed to salvage a baked potato from a friendly helper. I was torn between eating it or stashing it behind my knee as one does at an Irish point-to-point. We now crouched wetly in the moonlight. Someone started to sing, 'By the sea, by the beautiful sea,' and I looked around wildly for anyone who might be leaving in a car. At last I spied a Land Rover driving off, and begged a lift. 'We're full,' they said. 'You'll have to get in the back.' I clambered in, and what did I see but the remains of the clams, buttery corn on the cob, baby lobster, hard rolls and plates of sweet potatoes. Bumping along the potholed road back to the Vineyard I had the best, and possibly the last, clambake I would ever enjoy.

To Arrange a Clambake

The night before the feast make a small pit of sand and line it with rocks and flat stones. Build a fire and tend it through the day. By night-time the ash should be flat on the rocks. The stones and rocks are by now extremely hot. Then bank the fire and leave it. The next day, early in the morning, make a fire again on top of what is left.

The picnic consists of fresh lobsters, clams, corn cobs wrapped in foil (these used to be wrapped in vine leaves) and sweet potatoes baked in their jackets. Cover the whole thing with seaweed and then put a wet tarpaulin over the top and leave roughly from 9 a.m. until 10 p.m., by which time all should be ready and tender. The seaweed supplies the flavour, keeps the moisture in and steams all the seafood. Now we also add half a broiler chicken, again in layers of seaweed, and this is delicious. People lie in the grass around this non-smoking fire and drink draught beer or cider. It's an all-day event.

About Clambakes

Whatever the size of your bake, dig your clams the day before. Scrub them well to remove sand. Put them in a bucket, well covered with seawater. Add cornmeal, allowing ½ cup to 2 quarts (2.28 litres) water. The cereal helps rid the clams of sand and internal waste. Leave the clams in a cool place. Rinse and drain them just before using.

Clambake

(for 20 people)

200 soft-shell clams
50 hard-shell clams (optional)
4 dozen ears of corn
5 broiling chickens
10 sweet potatoes
20 frankfurters (optional)
20 1½ lb (700 g) lobsters or 5 pecks or an equivalent weight of soft-shell crabs
butter, melted
beer or cider
watermelon
coffee

Start preparations at least 4 hours before you plan to serve. Dig a sandpit 1 foot deep and 3½ feet across. Line it with smooth round rocks. Be sure the rocks have not been baked before. Have a wet tarpaulin – generous enough to overlap the pit area by 1 foot all round – and a few rocks handy to weight the edges. Build a fire over the rock surface, using hardwood, and keep feeding it for the next 2½ to 3 hours while the rocks are heating. Gather and wash about 4 bushels of wet rock seaweed. In fact, it is wise to soak the seaweed for at least 45 minutes before use. Have a pail of seawater at hand.

Partially husk the ears of corn. Do not pull them quite clean but leave on the last layer or two. Rip these back far enough to remove the silk. Then replace them, so the kernels are fully protected. Reserve the pulled husks.

Quarter the chickens. You may wrap the chicken pieces in

cheesecloth or divide the food into 20 individual cheesecloth-wrapped servings, so that each person's food can later be removed as one unit.

Scrub the lobsters or crabs.

Now you are ready to arrange for the 'bake'. Rake the embers from the hot stones, remove them from the pit and line it with the wet seaweed, covering the stones. The lining should be about 6 inches deep. Put over it, if you wish, a piece of chicken wire. If you haven't wrapped the individual servings in cheesecloth, pack the pit in layers. For added flavour, put down first a layer of hard-shell clams, then the frankfurters if you use them, then the lobsters or crabs, the chicken and the soft-shell clams, the sweet potatoes and the ears of corn. You may also put seaweed between the layers. Cover the layered food with the reserved corn husks and sprinkle the whole with the bucket of seawater. Quickly cover with the wet tarpaulin. Weight the tarpaulin down well with rocks. The whole should steam covered for about 1 hour. During the steaming, it will puff up, which is a sign of a satisfactory 'bake'. To test, lift the tarpaulin carefully at one corner so as not to get sand into the pit and see if the clams have opened. If so, the whole feast should be cooked just to the right point. Have handy plenty of towels and melted butter.

Serve with beer or cider, with watermelon and coffee to follow.

Tina Brown

Tina came out to Mustique when Colin was selling plots of land there to write a feature on him for *Tatler*. And when Princess Margaret and I went to stay with Drue Heinz in New York, Tina and her husband Harry Evans were frequent visitors. She's been incredibly kind and supportive to me, she interviewed me when *Whatever Next* was published, in a theatre in New York and it was a riot, we had great fun sparking off each other and she kindly threw a wonderful dinner party for me afterwards.

Picnic at Macaroni Beach
Tina Brown

My family was never big on picnics. To create a memorable picnic at least one person in the household has to exhibit an imaginative interest in food. My mother was a huge culinary failure, and my father was only invested in the sangria. All my memories of family picnic attempts at Wimbledon, Henley Royal Regatta and Glyndebourne are sodden with the inevitable British downpour, hunched under umbrellas in collapsible chairs next to our parked car with the boot open to protect the egg salad sandwiches.

But there is one picnic that left its mark on my memory. It was hosted for Princess Margaret at Macaroni Beach on Mustique, the private island in the Caribbean whose founding Prospero was Colin Tennant, later Lord Glenconner. (His wife Lady Anne – who wasn't there – is the curator of this book.)

The other guests – Reinaldo and Carolina Herrera, Brian Alexander, Roddy Llewellyn, and various villa owners – were all a bit bleary-eyed after one of Colin's costume bacchanalias at Basil's Bar the night before. Colin had plunged around the dance floor holding a fuzzy orange wig which he clapped on the head of anyone who didn't seem to be getting into the swing of things. 'There's no one this wig can't improve,' he cried, as Princess Margaret and Roddy hit the floor for a majestic rock and roll.

The next day HRH was worried that her singing performance had not been up to snuff. 'It was the organist who let you down, Ma'am,' said Tennant diplomatically. 'However, I've made enquiries this morning and the general feeling here is that you were much better than you thought.'

Seated at a trestle table covered by a sparkling white linen tablecloth, we all murmured our assent. The picnic was set up in the spiky shade of gently swaying palm trees on Macaroni's white sands, and like everything associated with Colin, was choreographed and catered to perfection. Groaning platters of Scottish salmon finger sandwiches with fragrant dill, mini Melton Mowbray pork pies, creamy devilled eggs, the yellowest of corn salads, the rubiest of small tomatoes, crisp, viridescent lettuce, and most mouthwatering of all, tiny sausages skewered on cocktail sticks just waiting to be devoured before the dessert finale of guava jam tarts. And then a searing cry emanated from Princess Margaret's direction. 'What! No mustard! How am I expected to eat sausages without mustard!' The whole party leapt to its feet in consternation.

To solve the problem, albeit five decades later, I consulted Chef Jason, who prepares exquisite al fresco lunches for the guests of Barry Diller and Diane von Fürstenberg aboard Mr Diller's yacht *EOS*. Jason kindly created this recipe for mustard.

Lavender Honey Mustard à la Mustique

- ¼ cup brown mustard seeds
- ¼ cup yellow mustard seeds
- ½ cup water
- ½ cup apple cider vinegar
- 1 teaspoon turmeric
- ¼ cup lavender honey
- 1 tablespoon of the most fresh lavender flowers one can find, lightly chopped

Place seeds, water and vinegar in a bowl for two days. Blend with all remaining ingredients after this time.

Bon appetit!

Cecilia McEwan and Jools and Christabel Holland

Parties at the McEwans' were legendary. Terence Stamp, Jean Shrimpton and, of course, Princess Margaret were among the guests they hosted at their house, Bardrochat near Glen in Scotland. They were a very glamorous family, seen as a Scottish version of the Kennedys. Cecilia was the daughter of an Austrian prince, but she married Alexander McEwan who had learnt how to play the Mississippi blues in America in the 1950s. Together with his brother Rory they formed a duo and became quite famous at the time, appearing on television here and on the Ed Sullivan show in the States. Parties often ended up in a singalong, whether at their house or when they came to Glen; it was all tremendous fun. As well as being the consummate hostess, Cecilia was also committed to charity work. In the sixties she'd worked with leprosy sufferers in Thailand and in the 1990s was part of an aid convoy to Bosnia during the war.

Rory McEwan's daughter, Christabel, has become a great friend. She married Jools Holland, who had also been a guest of the McEwans in Scotland. I love Christabel and Jools. I often say to Christabel, 'I go to bed with Jools whenever I can... (watching him on the television of course).' We go on holiday together every year in August, as guests of a Turkish friend who flies us all somewhere hot on a private jet. I'm very lucky to have young friends, as I get into my nineties most of my friends have died, so it's lovely to know a younger generation. When we are on the yacht our host has toys like jet skis to play with and Jools would say, 'Come on, Anne, let's go for a ride, I promise not to go too fast!' So I'd hop on. I'm rather fond of a photograph I have of myself on a jet ski clinging on to Jools for dear life!

I love the fact that I have picnics both from Cecilia and from her niece Christabel in the book.

Marchmont Picnic
Cecilia McEwan

The picnic for me conjures up idyllic scenes under trees, dappled shade, a rippling stream, with girls in muslin and men in panama hats. Baskets of food, French bread and white wine. This illusion has been spitefully dashed by the Scottish Border climate, where many a memorable picnic has been endured, huddled under the walls of Hermitage Castle, the beauty of which has been shrouded in mist, rain mingling with a fried egg sarnie, and a snell wind anaesthetising the fingers.

Picnics now usually take place on the lawn, where a quick dash for cover can be organised at a moment's notice. A table helps to stop any spillages brought on by uneven surfaces or a surfeit of Bloody Marys. Paper everything (no regrets) – cloth, plates, cups and napkins – and burn the lot at the end. A piece of lamb barbecuing, smelling of rosemary, garlic and cognac. Crisp lettuce, cut very thick, to dip in either dressing or fresh mayonnaise; a personal adaptation of a Spanish omelette, which can be cooked and remain in a quiche dish and be eaten with fingers. A terrine to slap on some French bread while waiting for the lamb to cook. Some radishes, some cream cheese with freshly chopped herbs, apples, butter, salt and a large pepper grinder.

Finally, vital to cooks and guests alike, a great deal of drink. Cold white wine, beer, cider and apple juice.

One eccentricity carried on from childhood at Marchmont is the marmalade sandwich – it has to be at every picnic. This may sound unappetising, but can be interesting if made with brown bread, butter and chunky marmalade. There has to be a plentiful supply as addicts will eat them throughout the picnic, beginning as a first course and finishing up what is left as a sort of pudding.

Papillon of Lamb for Barbecue (Mr McEwan's Special)

A small leg of lamb, boned by the butcher so that when opened flat it resembles the shape of a butterfly. Marinate in brandy, olive oil, rosemary, crushed garlic and pepper. Seal on each side on the barbecue and cook for around 20 minutes depending on the thickness of the meat. It should be pink in the centre when cooked. Cut on a bread board in slices like an entrecôte.

Terrine of Game or Veal

> 6–8 rashers streaky bacon 8 oz (225 g) pig's liver
> 1 small onion

    1 clove garlic
    8 oz (225 g) sausagemeat
    parsley, marjoram, thyme
    8 oz (225 g) pie veal or breasts of pheasant
    8 oz (225 g) pork fat
    salt and pepper

Preheat the oven to gas mark 4 (350°F, 180°C). Line a baking dish with bacon rashers. Mince the pork, liver, onion and garlic, add the sausage meat and herbs and mix well. Spread half the liver mixture over the bacon in the dish. Arrange strips of veal or pheasant on top. Cover with the remaining liver mixture. Cover the pan with foil.

Place in a larger dish containing water and cook for one hour. Turn out while still warm and drain excess fat.

A Cooling Water Picnic
Christabel and Jools Holland

We are the current custodians of the ruin of 14th century Cooling Castle and have recently dug out the moat. Hoping to unearth suits of armour left over from the siege by Thomas Wyatt in 1554, or carelessly misplaced bejewelled swords, or furiously refused engagement rings, we actually found miles of barbed wire and one remarkably well-preserved, hand-painted sign bearing the ominous warning: *Beware Falling Stones*.

Ignoring the advice, we have now taken to enjoying this newly created water world from a very un-medieval but marvellously practical modern pedalo that can carry a surprising number of adults and/or children with impressive stability.

In challenging times there is no antidote more enjoyable than a water picnic.

The calming effects of being afloat under the dappled shade of chestnut and willow, with frogs camouflaged to perfection causing shrieks of startled merriment as they leap out of our path, and huge silent fish slipping beneath us like submarines, alchemise into an enchanter's spell to soothe the nerves and raise the spirits.

Having experimented with various food styles, some of them, such as sandwiches and boiled eggs, have proved all too easy to collapse or slip out of small hands, and drop moatwards with a heart-stopping plop before the wails of disappointment.

These little savoury mouthfuls are quick to make, easy to handle and satisfyingly filling.

(Makes 24)

1 onion, chopped
4 eggs
250 ml (8 fl oz) milk
60 g (2 oz) flour
½ teaspoon baking powder
60 g (2 oz) grated cheddar cheese or feta
parsley, chopped
pine nuts
125 g (4 oz) butter

Baking tray for 12 muffins.

Oven gas mark 6 (190°C, 375°F) or top Aga oven. Put the onion, eggs, milk, flour, baking powder, cheese and parsley into a mixer.

Whizz it up for about 30 seconds. Melt a little knob of butter into each muffin hole, fill up to about two thirds and bake for 25–30 minutes.

You can add bits of crispy bacon or chopped sausage for carnivores.

Gaia Servadio

Life was always incredibly sociable when we were up at Glen. One of Colin's friends who lived up there was the art historian William Mostyn-Owen who was married to Gaia, an Italian writer, and they lived in one wing of Aberuchill Castle in Perthshire. I have vivid memories of a wonderful lunch there. We arrived as it was snowing, being Scotland it was practically dark by lunchtime, and Gaia had lit the whole house with candles. It was almost a theatrical experience driving up to the house in the snow with candles in all the windows. No one in Scotland would have thought of doing that but Gaia made it all quite magical. We had a wonderful Italian feast and the children were whisked away for lunch, which Colin thought was perfect. Gaia's daughter Allegra was briefly married to Boris Johnson and was a great friend of my ex-daughter-in-law Anastasia. But it was the memory of that fabulous lunch that encouraged me to ask her to write about a picnic for us and I love her idea of cooking the picnic in situ, taken from her Italian roots, and transferred to a Scottish setting.

Anne Glenconner

The Kingdom of Picnics
Gaia Servadio

My idea of picnicking has sprung from eccentric, distant roots.

When my sister and I were very small and when spring had settled on the Euganean hills, my father would assemble a few cooking pans and put them and myself on his bicycle. My sister had her own bicycle, something I didn't envy because it terrified me. The food for the picnic – and that was the excitement – was to be found and cooked in situ. While one of us assembled dry branches, the other would charm the friars of the Abbey of Chiaravalle, a dream of a Romanesque building, into selling us some of their freshly baked bread. The farmers would let us have a few eggs, still warm; in the fields we would gather rucola, that bitter, pungent leaf, and wild mint. And then we would cook.

Now that I have moved to the kingdom of picnics (Britain), my approach remains basically the same: to enjoy a picnic properly one should find the food for it, and cook it, on the spot. Not that I light a fire when I go to Glyndebourne, but I don't see the point of taking a lot of pre-cooked food, a lot of plates and a lot of people transferring it in order to eat.

My recipe for a Scottish picnic – my home is in Scotland, and most of my picnicking is done there – is as follows. A fair number of children and grown-ups, raw potatoes, salt, plenty of butter, bread and a frying pan. Very fresh trout (still alive if possible) in a plastic bag. Cheeses, thyme, pepper, knives, forks, matches and glasses. Despite the occasional tempest, downpour, gale, etc., the burns and the beauty of Scotland make it a superb picnicking land.

So now we select the ideal spot (of course, someone will discover that the next curve of the burn was better). The children gather stones and dry branches; the fire is lit at once, while volunteers look for chanterelles and ceps (*Boletus edulis*) and others clean the trout in the burn.

Stuff the trout with thyme, salt them and cook them directly on the burning wood (turning them after five minutes). The eggs should be fried in the frying pan with the chanterelles or ceps; the bread toasted on the hot stones with the cheese on top. Nothing tastes better than food cooked on wood.

Drink: water, Scottish water, absolute delight!

At the end of this picnic everybody will be dirty and exhausted. Weather permitting, a dip in the burn is recommended.

Rachel Johnson

I first met Rachel, a hugely talented author, broadcaster and television presenter, when she invited me to speak on her podcast, *Difficult Women*. We got along so well, and I thoroughly enjoyed meeting her. It was just before I visited America to promote *Whatever Next* and she offered to come with me on the tour as my 'Lady-in-Waiting' – she would have been perfect!

Picnics and Scones
Rachel Johnson

One summer we were in Scotland staying at my husband's family 'seat', Kelburn Castle, with many children and friends, among them Kate Bingham, the vaccine queen, a woman of relentless dash and drive.

She would make us bicycle up glens and hurl the bikes over barbed-wire fences, and swim in burns and lochs in our pants, play cricket and race on beaches, and one evening, she told the assembled company the plan for the morrow.

We would get up early and catch the eight o'clock ferry to Arran, pick up mountain bikes, then hide them in the brambles somewhere to climb Goat Fell on foot. 'It'll be fun,' she said, 'We'll take a picnic.'

After dinner, late, Kate and I mustered in the kitchen and made the most sumptuous picnic. We cut thick slices of wholemeal bread, buttered them, then layered slices of roast lamb, cheddar, chutney, and tomato. Each one was the size of a small brick, wrapped in cling film. We packed these with boiled eggs and jumbo slabs of Cadbury's Dairy Milk and water into a backpack that she would carry without complaint.

The only child of mine who would come was my oldest son Ludo, then a sleepy adolescent. As we ascended Goat Fell, having stowed our bikes, it was like climbing Kilimanjaro, only with midges. We trudged and trudged, munching the chocolate to keep us going, while the Bingham clan scampered ahead, declaiming sonnets and singing acapella.

We two were the last to summit and found everyone sitting about, in reverential silence as they rewarded themselves with the excellent lamb sandwiches. Kate handed me and Ludo ours and we settled by a trig point to tuck in. Ludo unwrapped his and sat, stunned for a moment, in contemplation not of the view (clouds of midges) but his sad fate, sandwich in hand.

At that moment a black Labrador ambled up and swiped Ludo's sandwich and wolfed it as easily as Timmy in *The Famous Five* disposing of a dish of strawberry ice cream. Ludo burst into tears. I gave him half of mine, and he has had a horror of picnics (and fell walking) ever since.

As we live on Exmoor, to me a picnic is portable food you can eat out of your hands and needs no embellishment. Pork pies. Sausage rolls. But above all, pasties (not pronounced 'parsties', please). A warm meat pasty or cheese pasty is the food of the gods, eaten halfway through a long walk along the Doone Valley or Valley of the Rocks, before a swim perhaps, knowing that a cream tea awaits you at the finishing post. '"Food always tastes better in the open air",' my father would quote a repeated line in *The Famous Five*, always adding, '"Said George wagging her tail",' and it does. One is hungrier and there's nothing I love more than feeling hungry and knowing I am about to scoff something sustaining and scrumptious, like an egg sandwich, say.

Though I am very lazy, I can knock up scones – which I regard as a vehicle for clotted cream and raspberry jam – in a jiffy. When it's not raining I take the tray out to the garden and we have picnic cream teas on the grass. Once the broadcaster and all-round goddess Emily Maitlis came to our farm for a snoop and stayed for tea and I'll always remember how she wanted her scone: 'Lots of clotted cream, please, and only a little bit of jam.'

I remind her of it sometimes. 'Only a little bit of jam eh, Maitlis?' and she will reply, 'And LOTS of clotted cream.'

Susanna Johnston

Zanna, as I always knew Susanna, was my husband Colin's first cousin; her mother and Colin's mother were sisters. I always said that one of the best things about marrying Colin was getting to know Zanna, we just clicked. We travelled quite a lot together to Thailand and Myanmar – or Burma as it then was. She was so full of ideas and so interested in everything, always fun to be around. She was a writer and wrote a marvellous book about the art historians Hugh Honour and John Fleming with whom she had lived in Italy for a while when she was much younger and completely fell in love with the country. She and her husband bought a beautiful house in Tuscany, near Lucca, and some of the picnics in this book are from friends who either stayed with her there or were invited for one of the wonderful long lunches she used to have. Italy was such a favoured holiday destination for us and our friends. I think it was a continuation of the time when artistocratic young men in the eighteenth century used to travel around Italy discovering its cultural highlights. The Grand Tour was seen as a rite of passage. Zanna used to drive down to their house in Italy for the summer, smoking all the way, with her husband Nicky, whom she adored. She'd been introduced to Nicky, who was an architect, by his great friend, Mark Boxer and they ended up living next to Mark and his then wife Arabella Boxer in London, which is how we asked Arabella to write for the *Picnic Papers*.

Picnic at Bagni du Lucca
Susanna Johnston

We drove along the Valley of the Serchio, which lies between the Apennines and the Appian Alps, towards Bagni di Lucca, a little spa beloved by English poets and writers throughout the centuries for its warm sulphur baths and for being permanently shaded by overhanging mountains and thick chestnut woods. We were making for the small Protestant cemetery where Ouida (the novelist Louise de la Ramée, who took her own childish mispronunciation of her first name as her nom de plume) lies buried. This cemetery is not easy to storm, and bribery and negotiation with the neighbours is needed.

Ouida died of pneumonia in the severe winter of 1909 at the age of sixty-nine and was buried at Bagni di Lucca after years of degradation and near-blindness, deserted by all but her faithful dog. The English consul of the time is said to have been moved by her bleak end and to have paid for her beautiful tomb in the style of the Della Quercia effigy of 1406 in the Duomo at Lucca. By the time we met our friends at the pretty iron gateway to the cemetery, the Tuscan heavens had opened. We pulled our coats over our heads, covered our baskets as best we could, and belted up the path to a small deserted chapel which, to our delight, turned out to be used for storing bales of hay. These we quickly rearranged to provide ourselves with table and benches – using rugs as a tablecloth. In no time we were very snug, looking out at a drenched Ouida and the over-hanging mountains half-hidden in mist and beating rain. Surrounded as we were by chestnut woods, it seemed appropriate to start with this soup, kept hot in a large thermos.

Chestnut Soup or Zuppa di Castagne

> 1 lb (450 g) chestnuts
> 2 oz (50 g) butter
> 2 onions, chopped
> 2 carrots, sliced
> 1 piece celery, sliced
> salt
> pepper
> 1 litre stock

Score the chestnuts on their rounded side and bake in a slow oven for 10 minutes. Peel while still warm. In the butter, brown the chopped onions, carrots and celery. Add the chestnuts, stock and seasoning. Cook for about 40 minutes until the chestnuts are completely tender and have started to break up. Put the soup through a sieve. Reheat and pour into large thermos.

Chocolate Truffles or Tartuffi di Cioccolata

> ½ lb (700 g) bitter chocolate
> 1 teaspoon milk
> 2 oz (50 g) butter
> 1 egg yolk

1 oz (25 g) cocoa

Melt the chocolate and milk in a double boiler. When smooth take it off the heat and work in the butter and egg yolk. Leave the mixture for 4 or 5 hours. Form into walnut shapes and coat with cocoa powder. These must be eaten within 4 hours and kept very cool. One tablespoon coffee powder can be added to vary the flavour when melting the chocolate.

Tessa Baring

Tessa was one of the group who used to gather at Zanna's house in Tuscany. Zanna had an Italian cook who would come in and prepare food for us and we used to head off to the Italian open-air market in the morning to buy what was required that day. I remember being asked to buy the mushrooms but there were hundreds of different kinds on display and I chickened out – there was no way I was going to be responsible for buying them in case everyone died and it was all my fault! But Tessa bravely volunteered to make the selection and we all survived. We always ate lunch outside under umbrellas, everyone had their children there, it was magical.

A Breakfast Picnic
Tessa Baring

The breakfast picnic is a tradition in my husband's family, a strange race of early risers. I recommend it particularly to people with the kind of small children who wake up at five o'clock on summer mornings and are horribly bored for hours before the day is allowed to begin.

Decide on a morning which is likely to be fine, and choose a place that is remote and beautiful but not too far off a road. These picnics are most fun if shared with friends, or with cousins as we used to. Each family should bring some of the food items, and for some reason it is particularly successful if the age range spans three generations. There is a feeling of excitement and exclusiveness at being the only people about so early in the morning, and someone is sure to remark that it is the most beautiful part of the day, and that other people are very stupid to miss it.

When you arrive at your chosen site, the first task is for children to find suitable sticks to light the campfire, and it adds to the sense of adventure if some 'wild' food is found, such as wild raspberries or, later in the year, mushrooms (but only if there is someone in the group who knows what they are looking for!). My mother-in-law has memories of breakfast picnics as a child, where the speciality was an omelette made from blackbirds' eggs stolen from the nest and cooked in a doll's frying pan. (There was more countryside to go round in those days and such a thing would not have been frowned upon as it would today.) Otherwise the ingredients are those of a normal old-fashioned English breakfast: bacon, fried eggs, fried bread (preferably brown and home-made), sausages and fried tomatoes, which are essential as they freshen up the otherwise rather greasy taste. Potato cakes also go down well early in the morning; they can be prepared in advance and brought in aluminium foil ready for frying.

It is important for someone to bring a frying pan, matches, newspaper, some form of cooking fat or oil, thermos flasks of coffee and orange juice for the children, plates, knives and forks and a few rugs, as the grass will be wet with dew. Also an oven

Susanna and me photographed when the original book
came out in 1983

Wicker hampers bearing culinary delights at a picnic with Princess Margaret
and friends in Norfolk

My photograph of George Christie who gamely jumped into the Ha-Ha at Glyndebourne

Arabella Boxer with one of her picnics for the air

Jasper Guinness with his 'Whoopee Picnic'

Colin, Roddy and Princess Margaret at one of the many parties on Mustique

Sandwiched between Mick Jagger and Rupert Everett in the mid 80's

Colin, Princess Margaret and me with friends eating macaroni on Macaroni Beach in Mustique

Having a ball on a jet ski with Jools Holland

Christabel Holland's cheese muffins at Cooling Castle

With my dear friend Margaret Vyner on one of our trips to India, shopping for fabrics in Jodhpur, taken by our friend and guide Mitch Crites

Rachel Johnson with friends Emily Maitlis and Alice Thomson enjoying homemade scones and tea in the garden

Long lunches with friends at Susanna's house in Italy

My grandson Euan with Susanna's wonderful Italian cook Bobbi

Freya Stark 'Dartmoor Picnic'

Cliff Parisi as a young boy

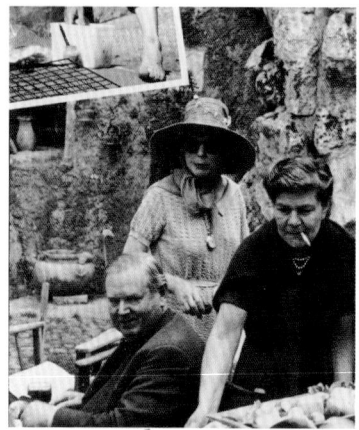
Evelyn Waugh, Lady Diana Cooper and Georgina Masson at a Picnic in Rome

Colette and Sam Clark picnicking with friends

Gamekeepers at Holkham pausing for sandwiches – the bowler hat was produced to fulfill an order from the Holkham estate for a hat to protect gamekeepers from low hanging branches, as their top hats kept being knocked off

The photograph I took of Valeria Coke with my cousin Eddie who became the 7th Earl of Leicester in 1994 with their children Thomas, Laura and Rupert by the Fountain of Perseus and Andromeda at Holkham, Norfolk

A cold day picnicking with my boys Henry and Charlie on the beach at Holkham

The Queen at a Poetry Together Mad Hatter's Tea Party with Gyles Brandreth's grandson, Rory playing the Mad Hatter and Hannah Grigg as Alice

Christopher, Amy and May on Boopa the elephant being led by Kent, sole beneficiary of my husband's Will, on St Lucia

Kelvin O'Mard with Henry in Norfolk

cloth is highly recommended, and something to deal with the inevitable burnt fingers.

When the cooking has been done and you are all sitting round the fire eating the most delicious breakfast you can remember, and feeling that you are the only people in the world, it's a wonderful time for conversation.

A Scottish Recipe for Potato Cakes

> 2 lb (900 g) potatoes, freshly boiled in their jackets
> 8 oz (225 g) self-raising flour
> salt

Sieve the potatoes on to a floured board, add the salt, and work in the flour by degrees, kneading lightly. Then roll out thinly, cut into rounds the size of a dinner plate, and cut each round into quarters.

Fry.

Michael Grant

Michael lived with his wife in a village near Lucca and was one of Zanna's lunch guests. Sometimes lunch would be at a long table under the fig tree in the garden where lovely ripe figs, if they hadn't been picked in time, would suddenly come plopping down onto the table, which was always laden with carafes of red and white wine and proscuitto and all manner of delicious Italian treats. But sometimes we would take a picnic into the countryside. We would borrow a donkey from the village and load it up with panniers containing the picnic and rugs and wander up into the hills. Obviously deciding where to stop was always a nightmare, 'Let's stop here,' someone would say. 'No, no. I think there's a better spot round the corner, until someone else would put their foot down and say, 'We're having it here, we're not going any further, the donkey is tired!'

Michael was a great classicist and wrote books on ancient Rome.

Anne Glenconner

The Picnics of the Ancient Romans
Michael Grant

Julius Caesar followed up the celebration of his triumphs over his enemies by presiding – sweating profusely, we are told – over an open-air dinner in the public squares of Rome, attended by many tens if not hundreds of thousands of Romans, who drank a good Italian wine (Falernian) and ate, among other things, six thousand eels 'lent' to Caesar by a former political opponent. The dictator liked doing things on a large scale, and this may have been the biggest picnic of all time (picnic? Yes, according to the *Concise Oxford Dictionary*, 'pleasure party including meal out of doors').

Queen Cleopatra did not attend Caesar's party because she was not in Rome, although she arrived shortly afterwards. But if she had been at the dinner she would surely have felt like one of her royal Greek forbears, Queen Arsinoe III of Egypt, who described the picnickers at Alexandria's Feast of Flagons as 'a squalid kind of party – a mixed crowd gorging up stale food'.

Arsinoe would scarcely have been better pleased if she had attended some of the numerous similar festivals in Italy, which gave the opportunity for a good deal of fairly unrestrained eating and drinking. For example, at the annual Festival of Anna Perenna, on 15 March, people camped out with their girlfriends in tents or huts of leafy boughs or reeds, and everyone drank themselves silly. At the Hilaria, the spring festival of the Great Mother, it was the custom to offer the goddess an extraordinarily pungent, garlicky salad ('Its powerful whiff smites the nostrils,' remarked a poet), and no doubt the revellers ate the leftovers. But it was at the various Italian harvest and grape harvest celebrations that the most extensive open-air eating and drinking took place. The emperor Elagabalus once took his court to one of these wine festivals. An outdoor occasion of such a kind did not, perhaps, give him an opportunity for some of his most exquisite alleged touches of banqueting humour, such as letting down a mass of violets and other flowers from the ceiling in such quantities that the guests were smothered to death, but nevertheless we are given a lively account of the coarse talk with which he saw fit to enliven the occasion.

The shepherds in Virgil's *Eclogues* invest the idea of *déjeuner sur l'herbe* with a far more idyllic, romantic glow. However, the *Eclogues* were written not for shepherds but for highly sophisticated Romans: and such Romans, although they were prepared to read about such matters – and had (indoors) adopted the uncomfortable eastern and Greek practice of eating lying down – would mostly have endured almost any torture rather than share the discomforts of what we understand by a picnic. After all, one did not *have* to eat completely out of doors. True, as recent discoveries have shown, it was possible to eat at pleasant little dining places in a Pompeii vineyard, under a pergola. But the architects of the grand houses and villas in the area were adept at distributing a number of indoor dining rooms, suited to the various seasons, at various strategic points of the building, including summer rooms that were *very nearly* out of doors, opening alluringly upon elegant gardens (not upon untutored nature, except for the occasional seascape). A rich, fastidious late Roman, Sidonius Apollinaris, describes such a room, though while gushing about the view he also does not fail to mention a 'glittering sideboard' – and a staircase especially designed to avoid the slightest physical exertion.

However, an earlier Roman, Pliny the Younger, at his country house on the borders of Tuscany and Umbria, actually entertained in his garden, completely al fresco, beside a marble basin filled with water: 'The preliminaries and main dishes for dinner are placed on the edge of the basin, while the lighter ones float about in vessels shaped like birds or little boats.' (Presumably slaves stood around with rakes to pull them in.) For whenever Romans could be lured outside to eat in the open air, they rather liked to have a watery setting. In the reign of Claudius, for example, a lot of people dined out to help the emperor celebrate the opening of a channel between a lake and a river. But the water overflowed, the picnickers got the shock of their lives, and the sponsor of the project ran into trouble.

More successful, in its way, was a rather unusual outdoor party given by Nero's appalling adviser Tigellinus on an artificial lake (or, according to another account, in a theatre specially flooded for the purpose). Tacitus reported it thus:

> The entertainment took place on a raft, towed about by other vessels, with gold and ivory fittings. Their gay oarsmen were assorted according to age and speciality. Tigellinus had also collected birds and animals from remote countries, and even the creatures of the ocean. On the quays were brothels stocked with high-ranking ladies. Opposite them could be seen naked prostitutes, indecently posturing and gesturing. At nightfall, the woods and houses nearby echoed with singing and blazed with lights...

The Romans, if they had to picnic, also liked to use grottoes or caves for the purpose. Some garden dining rooms at Pompeii are artfully designed to look as if that was what they were. But you could also eat in real caves. The Emperor Tiberius did this on one occasion, with results even more disastrous than those which usually attend picnics: a fall of rock occurred that would have killed him, if his friend Sejanus had not interposed his body as a shield – an action that proved beneficial to his future career.

The wine drunk at these out-of-door meals, or indeed at any Roman party, was quite likely to include a tincture not only of resin (as in Greece today) or lime or even ashes (to counteract acidity) but also salt, almonds or goats' milk (to add maturity and flavour); and it was always possible that a red-hot iron had been dipped in it as well, for the same purpose. One also wonders, scanning the pages of Petronius' *Dinner of Trimalchio* and the scarcely less startling *Cookery Book of Apicius*, whether any of the more peculiar dishes described in these works made their appearance at a Roman picnic. Certainly, whatever meat or fish was provided, it would not have been served in any simple form (this elaborateness was no trouble to a Roman cook, who habitually produced his results, however complicated, on mobile, portable, sometimes unroofed charcoal stoves and tripods and gridirons).

Before sewing up your roast dormouse, for example, you ought to stuff it with minced pork and pound it with pepper, pine kernels, asafoetida or 'stinking mastic' (resinous gum smelling of garlic) and *liquamen*. *Liquamen* was the basis of *garum*, one of the very sharp sauces with which the Romans liked to drench every dish, partly because things went bad so quickly. According to one of its recipes, *garum* consisted basically of the chopped, pounded and crushed entrails of sprats and sardines, beaten into a fermented pulp (this is *liquamen*), which was left to evaporate for six weeks and then filtered through a perforated basket into a receptacle. The poet Martial, casting around for words to describe a friend's bad breath, can only remark that it would make even the strongest scent stink like *garum*; here, at least, is one argument in favour of outdoor picnics.

Martial speaks of fans of peacock feathers to keep flies away. But to the Emperor Domitian the flies that are always such a bore at picnics might actually have been an incentive to join in, because he liked having them around, amusing himself by catching them and cutting them to pieces with a specially sharpened metal pen. However, a picnic would not have been a possible milieu for his well-known party joke – serving the petrified senators who were his guests with black dishes and miniature gravestones inscribed with their names – because this inimitably humorous prank required indoor accommodation, with ceiling, walls and floor painted an equally funereal black. However, the insertion of Domitian into a discussion of picnics is probably irrelevant, since that emperor is even less likely than most other prominent Romans ever to have gone on one – and certainly not on a water picnic, since we are told that, although he enjoyed solitary walks, there were certain outdoor noises, notably the splash of oars, that he found intolerably irritating.

Hugh Honour

Zanna met Hugh Honour and his partner John Fleming when she was a teenager living in Italy and, she said, they sort of adopted her, as you might a stray dog. Hugh was a world-renowned art historian who, together with John, wrote the famous *World History of Art*. They lived in a villa called Villa Marchio just outside Lucca, and Zanna ended up buying her house near them. It was always wonderful going there as they were interesting, and excellent conversationalists, but they were pretty eccentric and it wasn't the cleanest house. They had a rather ancient and slow help they called Speedy who knocked us up food, and you tried not to think about the mice you'd seen running around in the kitchen as you ate the pasta she'd prepared. Zanna's husband Nicholas had also been a friend of Hugh's at Cambridge so that helped to cement the friendship further, and she ended up writing a memoir about them. Hugh's picnic is wonderfully literary, based on the novel *Marius the Epicurean* by Walter Pater, and I think conjures up a sense of all the literary figures who travelled through that part of the world.

Anne Glenconner

A White Picnic
Hugh Honour

My ideal of a perfect picnic belongs to the 1950s, not later or earlier. Childhood treats were all very well in a Betjemanesque way. I too 'used to picnic where the thrift/grew deep and tufted to the edge'. But today, driving along the autoroute south of Lyon, I read the signs '*Pique-nique jeux d'enfants*' as a warning rather than an invitation – though the phrase does have a ring of Verlaine about it. Most of my picnics nowadays are eaten on journeys across Europe by road. The company, limited to a maximum of four, is always that of old friends. The food, bought in the town where we spent the previous night, is also well tried – in Italy cold roast suckling pig and the best baked bread to be found anywhere in Europe now (much better than in France where it used to be so delicious), in Spain strongly flavoured ham, in Germany liver sausage, in France a selection of pâtés and galantines and *oeufs en gêlée*. These picnics are no more than brief affairs, however, intervals in a long drive, and never quite match up to my or any other ideal. The *oeufs en gêlée* too often prove to be hard-boiled, not *mollets*. The place where we stop attracts others almost immediately, and seldom seems in retrospect as congenial as the one we had passed only a few minutes earlier or the one we noticed soon afterwards.

For me the perfect picnic must be incidental, just part of a journey through country beautiful in itself and, if possible, with literary or historical associations as well. My ideal picnic began to form twenty-five years or so ago when I lived in Percy Lubbock's villa, Gli Scafari, near Lerici – a house of cool marmorial beauty perched on a rocky promontory above the crystalline blue of the still unpolluted Mediterranean, with a wide view of distant islands and the little fishing village of Porto Venere on the northern arm of the Gulf of La Spezia. The air was drowsy with literary associations. Percy himself had been at Cambridge with E.M. Forster – 'Poor old Morgan,' as he often remarked, 'he never knew quite the "right" people.' Later he had been a disciple of Henry James, whose voice and conversation he could mimic when well-primed after dinner and, for a time, one of Edith Wharton's 'young men' – though he was banished from her little court when he married another wealthy cosmopolitan blue-stocking. Only a few hundred yards away D.H. Lawrence had spent the winter of 1913–14 in a four-room pink cottage on the shore of 'a little tiny bay half shut in by rocks, and smothered by olive woods that slope down swiftly'. Beneath Gli Scafari there was a huge, arching grotto, one of those, we liked to think, that Shelley had explored by boat during the last weeks of his life when he lived at San Terenzo on the other side of Lerici. Byron, on his way from Pisa to Genoa in October 1823, stopped at Lerici for a few nights and made himself ill by swimming far out to sea with Trelawny and eating a large dinner while treading water – one of the most bizarre picnics on record. Next year he was to sail along the same coast on his last voyage, to Missolonghi. But, as we watched from the loggia the passage of shipping out at sea or making for harbour at La Spezia or Porto Venere, there was another figure from the past who haunted our imaginations – Walter Pater.

I had first read *Marius the Epicurean* at school and thought it, as did the young Max Beerbohm, a marvellous 'tale of adventure, quite as fascinating as *Midshipman Easy*, and far less hard to understand because there were no nautical terms in it'. At Lerici I found myself near Marius's country. His villa, White Nights, was among the hills a few miles inland. Pater wrote that 'the traveller, descending from the slopes of Luna even as he got his first view of the "Port-of-Venus" would pause by the way, to read the face, as it were, of so beautiful a dwelling place, lying away from the white road, at the point where it began to descend somewhat steeply to the marshland below'. Each of the windows of Marius's tower chamber framed a landscape, 'the pallid crags of Carrara, like wildly twisted snowdrifts above the purple heath; the distant harbour with its freight of white marble going to sea; the lighthouse temple of "Venus Speciosa" on its dark headland, amid the long-drawn curves of white breakers'. The description is circumstantial enough to suggest that Pater, who could have passed this way when he went to Pisa, had a particular spot in mind. To find it became the object of many excursions and picnics.

Near the little village of Fosdinovo there are several places which almost match Pater's description. From there one can see the Carrara mountains, uncannily like those in the background to the *Mona Lisa*, which inspired one of Pater's over-familiar purple passages. Glimpses may be caught of an ancient amphitheatre among vineyards, all that remains above ground of the city of Luni from which Carrara marble was exported throughout the Roman Empire. But to find a point from which Porto Venere can also be seen is difficult. I never succeeded in locating it. If found, this would be the place for the perfect, the truly Epicurean picnic.

Special food would, of course, be eaten, food of a preciosity to suit the occasion and predominantly white. We should begin with fish, cold fillets of sole or shelled scampi and a very pale mayonnaise. Then there might be chicken breasts or quails, stuffed with white truffles and wrapped in the most delicately streaked bacon, lightly fried, accompanied by a white salad such as is sometimes served in Italy in early spring – raw fennel cut into little strips, celery, chicory and paper-thin flakes of turnip sprinkled over with violet flowers to delight both eye and palate. To end we should have a cheese mousse of the type the cook at Gli Scafari used to prepare, firm yet crumbly to the fork and wonderfully light, composed mainly of ricotta (ewe's milk cheese) but according to a recipe I have never been able to trace. We should drink a dry white wine, Verdicchio from the Marche. And afterwards, until the sun sinks into the sea, we would read Pater's 'oft-read tale' again, from the edition printed on handmade paper with title page designed by Herbert Horne, the biographer of Botticelli and one of the last Anglo-Italians of whom Pater might have wholly approved. But the place has not been, and may never be, found. So my perfect picnic remains an untarnished ideal – forever cold and still to be enjoyed.

William Weaver

William was a friend of Zanna's. He was an English translator of modern Italian literature and part of the Italian clan who also had a house in Tuscany, as he describes in this picnic.

A Spontini Picnic
William Weaver

I love music and I love food. Normally I do not enjoy them together. I have walked out of restaurants in protest (ineffectual, I fear) against their muzak or their pianist; I have asked hostesses to turn off the radio or the gramophone; and it is years since I have picnicked on a beach, because the invasion of transistors has succeeded in spoiling that pleasure. So naturally, on a picnic, I would ban any kind of music, reproduced or live (the sight of a guitar immediately suggests the drawl of folk songs and, just as immediately, provokes anticipatory indigestion).

Still, I must admit that one of the most enjoyable al frescos I have had was, in fact, a musical evening on my own terrace. It was several years ago, and Italian Radio was broadcasting *Agnes von Hohenstausen*, a rarely performed opera by Spontini, starring Monserrat Caballe. I learned about the broadcast only after I had invited a few friends to supper.

Fortunately the guests were all music lovers and, in fact, as eager to hear the opera as I was. The radio, however, and the taping equipment were in my cluttered study, which was not the ideal room for dining in. But just outside the study window there is a terrace, with a pergola of grapevines, a table and some chairs. The loudspeakers in the study could be shifted to the window, so that they could be heard by listeners on the terrace. The food, which was cold, had been prepared in the afternoon. It was placed on the table so that guests could help themselves, and they were asked to be on hand a good half hour before the opera was to begin. So we had time for a glass of wine. After the music started, the only noise was an occasional gurgle of more wine being poured and perhaps one or two clanks of dropped cutlery. There were long intervals between the acts, so we could enjoy more talk. And then, when it was over, we had a final glass and exchanged impressions.

We ate one of the many Italian kinds of cold pasta (which I know sounds revolting to the Anglo-Saxon, but is actually delicious), a cold *frittata* – by cold I mean room temperature – and a salad and cheeses and fruit (perhaps grapes from above our heads). And, to be sure, Spontini. Just the right composer for a Tuscan picnic. Verdi would have demanded our total attention, distracting us from the food; and perhaps another composer – I'll name no names – would not have prevented us from talking.

Cold Chitarrucci

>2 lb (900 g) tomatoes
>1 cup of basil and marjoram, finely chopped
>salt, pepper
>olive oil
>1 lb (450 g) pasta (if possible chitarrucci – the
>   squared-off fine spaghetti)

Prepare the sauce one day before. Peel, seed and chop the tomatoes. Put in a bowl and add the chopped marjoram, basil, plenty of salt and pepper. Leave it to sweat. Drain. Add the oil.

Next day, cook the pasta in the ordinary way. Cool by tossing well in the sauce.

Frittata

>small onion
>1 tablespoon olive oil
>2 large tomatoes, peeled and chopped
>1 lb (450 g) courgettes, chopped
>8 eggs
>1 tablespoon grated Parmesan
>1 tablespoon flour
>salt, pepper
>6–7 leaves basil, chopped
>6–7 leaves celery, chopped

Chop the onion and fry gently in the oil. Add the tomatoes and courgettes. Cook on a medium heat for about 20 minutes in a frying pan. Mix the eggs with the cheese, flour, salt and pepper.

When the courgettes and tomatoes are cooked, take them off the heat and add to the egg mixture. Stir quickly. Add the basil and celery leaves. Put back on a medium heat and cook on both sides, turning with the help of a plate. Cool. If the frittata breaks, beat another egg and use for repair work.

John Chancellor

Zanna's brother, John Chancellor, wrote about a country churchyard picnic for us. His daughter Anna Chancellor is an actress who is perhaps best known for playing Duckface in *Four Weddings and a Funeral*.

A Country Churchyard Picnic
John Chancellor

It might be thought that a churchyard is a macabre venue for a picnic. Picnics are, after all, supposed to be cheerful occasions, when you are not expected to entertain thoughts of death. The most fearless and unimaginative of us might hesitate before spreading the contents of a picnic basket upon a tombstone. Who knows how its ghostly occupant would take it?

Some churchyards are more inviting than others. An example of a friendly churchyard is that in the village of Selborne in Hampshire, the home of the immortal Gilbert White. It is universally agreed that Gilbert White has given delight to generations; but who he was and the exact nature of this 'delight' is known to very few. Nevertheless the book, upon which rests his unshakeable yet elusive fame, has been reprinted almost every year since it was published in 1789, with the title *The Natural History and Antiquities of Selborne*.

The opportunity offered itself one Sunday in September to make an expedition to Selborne. My son was at school at Winchester, where once or twice a term I took him out. These occasions were pleasant enough, but shockingly expensive. I learned there that it was not only in London that the price of a meal in a restaurant was scandalous. Admittedly, he did not make a point of going for the cheaper items, and I was amazed at the number of gin and tonics that he managed to drink. It was my sister who, horrified at seeing me pay over a vast sum for one of these Winchester meals (two of her daughters were there also), insisted that the next time we took the boy out, it would be a picnic or nothing.

So we found ourselves on that Sunday in September making our way from Winchester to Selborne. All the members of the party were united by the haziness of their knowledge as to who or what Gilbert White was. My son, furthermore, had the temerity to doubt the extent of the delight that White had given later generations. These doubts were, alas, to intensify as the day went on.

We passed through many a charming village before reaching our destination. This was the moment to prepare my captive companions for the great experience ahead of them, to acquaint them with the 'genius' of Gilbert White. On that very week, two hundred years earlier, he had made these observations in his journal:

Black snails lie out, and copulate. Vast swagging clouds... red-breasts feed on elderberries, enter rooms, and spoil the furniture... women make poor wages in their hop-picking. Housed all my potatoes, and tied up my endives... swallows hawking about very briskly in all the moderate rain... then we called loudly thro' the speaking trumpet to Timothy (his tortoise), he does not seem to regard the noise.

There were few swagging clouds on that particular Sunday, and we lacked the acuteness of observation to notice how many black snails were copulating.

The entries in his journal explain perhaps why Gilbert White occupies so firm a place in the heart of the normal, wholesome Englishman. The English like their heroes to be simple and unaffected, to be stay-at-home and unambitious, and to be disinterested in the activities they pursue, thinking of neither gain nor fame. Gilbert White was all these things. He spent his whole life in the same house at Selborne; he never aspired to be more than a curate, and he recorded meticulously, day after day, what he saw happening in the countryside around him. All this he had put down in *Selborne*, that little-read classic of English literature, a copy of which I had not forgotten to bring on this expedition. It was my plan to read aloud during our picnic one or two of its imperishable passages.

We entered the village, at the end of which we came to Selborne church and churchyard, described by White as 'very scanty... such a mass of mortality that no person can be interred there without disturbing or displacing the bones of his ancestors'. We squeezed ourselves between several tombstones, very near the splendid yew tree with an enormous girth which White measured every year in his meticulous and disinterested way. He also observed that it was a male tree.

Whilst the others tucked in, I expatiated on the greatness and modesty of Gilbert White and began to read aloud from the famous book. Maybe I chose one of the less stimulating passages – it was about the diversity of soils in the district – or maybe the solemnity of the occasion overcame them, or maybe it was my sister's delicious food, but when I looked up my companions were, one and all, dozing among the tombstones.

Cauliflower Salad

> 1–2 cauliflowers
> salt
> pepper
> cayenne
> 2 eggs
> 1 teaspoon mixed mustard
> 1 oz (25 g) sugar
> 1 oz (25 g) butter
> 4 tablespoons milk
> 3 tablespoons vinegar

Cook the cauliflowers in boiling salted water. Don't overcook – let them retain a little 'bite'. Then leave them in a colander to drain. Divide into small florets and place in a salad bowl. Season well with pepper, salt and cayenne and make the following sauce.

Beat the eggs in a double boiler. Add a level teaspoon of salt, the mustard, sugar, butter, milk and vinegar. Stir over boiling water till it thickens. Then pour over the salad, or bottle and pour over before it is served.

Mint Lemonade

> 4 large lemons
> 8 oz (225 g) sugar
> 1 handful fresh mint
> ice cubes
> 4 bottles ginger ale

Squeeze the lemons and strain the juice. Add the sugar and stir until dissolved. Put into a chilled thermos with mint and some ice cubes. Pack the chilled ginger ale separately in an insulated bag and add just before serving.

Clara Johnston

Clara and I share a love of India. She is Zanna's daughter, who I've known forever. Like lots of young people she travelled in India and knew Bubbles who was the Maharaja of Jaipur. I knew Bubbles too. He gained that nickname apparently from all the champagne that was drunk to celebrate his birth as he was the first male heir to be born to the Maharaja of Jaipur for generations.

A Maharaja's Picnic Tea
Clara Johnston

One afternoon when nothing much was happening in the City Palace, Bubbles, the Maharaja of Jaipur, decided to take us to see his father's old shooting lodge about fifteen miles outside Jaipur. A picnic was prepared and put into the back of the American jeep along with Clare Steel, the uniformed bodyguard, and myself.

In Jaipur, Bubbles is still thought of as the king and those who recognised the T-shirted driver clasped their hands together and bowed as we drove by.

Across a plain, along a thin, straight road, we passed ox-drawn carts brimming with hay and people and stopped for a moment at a lake which stretched for miles without so much as a ripple on its polished surface.

Later the land became hillier and the vegetation more dense. Just before we reached a great dam, Bubbles turned down a driveway lined with rambling shrubs. At the gate two octogenarian servants tumbled down the steps to greet us, as if our arrival had awoken them from a deep sleep.

The house had not been visited for some time and smelled of dust and mothballs. Built in the thirties, it looked like an Italian villa with pastel yellow stuccoed walls, balconies, shuttered windows and a loggia. The house had been used as a shooting lodge for the surrounding area and the hall was lined with stuffed tigers, bears and lions.

Below the front of the house was a stone hideout with square peepholes. Years ago the sport was to tie a bull to the hideout and wait for a tiger to approach. Those who were brave enough watched the event from within, while the rest watched safely from the house.

We sat, unthreatened by tigers, in the garden and the aged servants spread a white linen tablecloth over a round wooden table in the centre of the lawn. The picnic, a mixture of traditional English sandwiches and Indian spices, was spread out on the table by the bodyguard: cucumber sandwiches, spiced chicken, poppadoms, curd raitas and sweets. We drank tea out of a thermos – a picnic item inherited from the English – and watched the sun set over the lake.

Curd (Yoghurt) Raitas

> 1 pint (450 ml) plain yoghurt
> juice of half a lemon
> 2 cloves of garlic (crushed)
> chopped mint leaves
> finely chopped fresh green chilli

Pour the yoghurt into a bowl and beat in the rest of the ingredients. For variations you can add to taste: 1 teaspoon paprika, a pinch of cayenne, a pinch of coriander, coriander leaves or a pinch of cumin. Other ingredients such as raisins, sultanas, sliced bananas, grated carrots, chopped nuts or diced boiled new potatoes can be added. You can make it into a salad by adding raw vegetables.

Poppadoms

Some of the ingredients for poppadoms are not available in England so I have adapted it slightly.

> 3–4 tablespoons flour
> salt
> caraway seeds
> a little mild paprika
> cream or milk

Season the flour with salt and add caraway seeds and red pepper. Mix with cream or milk to a stiff paste. Knead well, roll out a little, cut into cubes of 1–1½ inches (2½–3¾ cm) diameter. Take each cube, roll it and fold it and roll it again, finally beating it with a rolling pin until it is paper thin and the size of a side plate. Prick each slice all over with a fork, lay on a greased and floured baking sheet and bake for three minutes or so in a very hot oven. The poppadoms should blister and be very thin and crisp.

Patrick Leigh Fermor

Patrick Leigh Fermor was terribly good looking, rather a Byronesque character, and I think we were all secretly a bit in love with him. In addition to cutting an extremely glamorous figure as a writer and explorer he was also very charming. He had been in the Special Operations Executive in Crete during the second world war and my father-in-law, who was in charge of the SOE, told me how incredibly brave Patrick was. He organised resistance to the occupation on the island and oversaw the capturing and expulsion of the German commander there. He also wrote about the islands of the West Indies and came to Mustique during the very early days when there was no electricity or running water, but of course he was used to all of that and didn't mind a bit.

The Dales of Moldavia
Patrick Leigh Fermor

It may be rash to intrude this Rumanian feast where so many literary cornucopias are pouring their bounty; for it is the day and the occasion that single out this one, and shadow steals over substance here and veils every memory of what there actually was to eat. (We had set out to pick mushrooms, but they were for dinner.)

The picnic baskets may have contained all sorts of Moldowalkechian wonders – *sarmali* wrapped in vine leaves, fragrant *mititei*, chicken croquettes as light as feathers, a *sterlet* from the Pruth, perhaps, or even, and by the ladleful, wonderful Black Sea caviar from Vâlcov in the Danube delta, on the fringes of Bessarabia; turkey in aspic, almost certainly. Apart from fine indigenous cooking this country seemed to be the meeting place of all that was most delicious in old Russia, Poland, Hungary, Mitteleuropa, France, the Balkans and the Levant. The picnic would have been more likely to start with fierce Moldavian *raki* than with a milder southern *tzuica* of distilled plums; excellent white and red wines, stored in tortuous catacombs, would have accompanied it throughout.

The point of departure was an old and many-legended Cantacuzene country house with inhabitants of indescribable charm. It lay at the heart of a once large but now much reduced estate in High Moldavia, and the time was September 1939. Apart from the two sisters who were our hostesses and their family, there was also, for the summer, Prince Matila Ghyka and three other young English people. (I had become a sort of fixture.) Matila Ghyka, traveller, diplomat, well-known writer on aesthetics – *Le Nombre d'Or, Sortilèges du Verbe*, etc. – and a gastronome famous for his encyclopaedic approach to life, would certainly have had a hand in the planning.

It was a summer of unparalleled beauty and remoteness, but the months passed too fast; the crops were in and the storks were gathering before heading south; and suddenly, not unannounced, the evil omens had begun to multiply quickly, until all seemed black. To forget and exorcise for a day the growing assembly of trouble we set off, on 2 September, to pick those mushrooms in a wood about ten miles away, some of us in an old open carriage, some on horseback; through the vineyards where the grapes were almost ready to be harvested and pressed, and out into the open country. The clearings in the wood, when we arrived, were studded with our quarry. Alighting and dismounting, we scattered in a competitive frenzy, reassembling soon with our baskets full to the brim. In the glade of this mysterious wood, with the tethered horses grazing and swishing their tails under the oak branches, the picnic spun itself out. Soon it was late afternoon and all the bottles were empty and the old Polish coachman was fidgeting the horses back into the shafts and fastening the traces. The ones on horseback set off by a different way. We raced each other across the mown slopes of the vast hayfields and galloped in noisy and wine-sprung zigzags through the ricks and down a wide valley and up again through another oak spinney to the road where the carriage, trailing a long plume of dust, was trotting more sedately home, and reined in alongside.

The track followed the crest of a high ridge with the dales of Moldavia flowing away on the either hand. We were moving through illimitable sweeps of still air. Touched with pink on their undersides by the declining sun, which also combed the tall stubble with gold, one or two shoals of mackerel cloud hung motionless in the enormous sky. Whale-shaped shadows expanded along the valleys below, and the spinneys were sending long loops of shade downhill.

The air was so still that the smoke from Matila Ghyka's cigar hung in a riband in the wake of our cavalcade; and how clearly the bells of the flocks, which were streaming down in haloes of golden dust to the wells and the brushwood folds a few ravines away, floated to our ears. Homing peasants waved their hats in greeting, and someone out of sight was singing one of those beautiful and rather forlorn country songs they call a *doina*. A blurred line along the sky a league away marked the itinerary of the deserting storks. Those in the carriage below were snowed under by picnic things and mushroom baskets and bunches of anemones picked in the wood. It was a moment of peace and tranquillity and we rode on in silence towards the still far-off samovar and the oil lamps and heaven knew what bad news. The silence was suddenly broken by an eager exclamation from Matila.

'Oh look!' he cried. One hand steadied the basket of mushrooms on his lap, the other pointed at the sky into which he was peering. High overhead some waterbirds, astray from the delta, perhaps, or from some nearby fen, were flying in a phalanx. (I shall have to improvise names and details here, for precise memory and ornithological knowledge both fail me. But the gist and the spirit are exact.)

'Yes,' he said, 'it's rather rare; the *Xiphorhyncus paludinensis minor*, the *glaivionette*, or Lesser Swamp Swordbill – *Wendischer Schwertvogel* in German, *glodnic* in Moldavian dialect; I believe the Wallachians call it *spadună de baltă*. Varieties are dotted about all over the world but always in very small numbers. They live in floating nests and have a very shrill ascending note in the mating season.' He whistled softly once or twice. 'Their eggs are a ravishing colour, a lovely lapis lazuli with little primrose speckles. They have been identified with the Stymphalian birds that Hercules killed, and there's a mention of them in Lucian's *Dialogues* and in Pliny the Elder, and I think in Oppian... The ancient Nubians revered them as minor gods and there's supposed to be one on a bas-relief at Cyrene; there's certainly a flight of them in the background of a *Journey of the Magi* by Sassetta – he probably saw them in the reeds of Lake Trasimene, where they still breed; and the chiefs of two tribes on the Zambezi wear robes of their tail feathers for the new moon ceremonies. Some people,' he continued, with a slight change of key, 'find them too fishy. It's not true, as I learnt years ago near Bordeaux. On a spit, over a very slow fire – of hornbeam twigs, if possible – with frequent basting and plenty of saffron, *glaivionette à la landaise* can be delicious... Alas: I've only eaten it once...'

His dark eyes, a-kindle with memory, watched the birds out of sight across the dying sky, and we all burst out laughing. The cosmic approach... It had been a happy day, as we had hoped, and it had to last us for a long time, for the next day's news scattered this little society for ever.

Penelope Chetwode

Penelope and my aunt Sylvia used to head off to Italy and Spain on adventures with ponies. Penelope was a travel writer and my aunt's best friend who used to come up to Norfolk to stay. I remember Sylvia telling me that on the first of their trips, before the ponies, they headed off to Rome in a Mini Minor. My aunt asked Penelope where she had booked for them to stay – certain that there was some lovely little hotel or guest house to look forward to – whereupon Penelope told her she must be quite mad, that she never stayed in hotels and had a tent in the back of the car. They spent ages putting up this awful wonky tent and Penelope got out a little stove to boil something up to eat; it was not what my aunt had in mind, she liked a comfortable bed. After two or three days my aunt said she was taking herself off to an hotel whether Penelope wanted to go with her or not! Despite this unpromising start, Sylvia carried on travelling with her and they loved exploring together. Penelope was married to the poet John Betjeman but after a while they separated and he lived with Lady Elizabeth Cavendish in London, who was responsible for introducing

Princess Margaret to Tony Armstrong-Jones, whilst Penelope lived near Hay-on-Wye.

Suprême de Volaille with St George in Cappadocia
Penelope Chetwode

After an interval of thirty years, I returned to India in 1963 by the overland route. A young doctor friend bought a second-hand Volkswagen Dormobile from a farmer near Wantage and proceeded to make a green roll-up tent on his mother's sewing machine – which has never worked since. The tent, fixed to the roof of the vehicle, could be unrolled and set up as a roomy lean-to shelter within five minutes of arriving at any campsite. The cooking was done in it on two primus stoves, and there was room for three people to sleep on the ground while two of us slept in the Dormobile.

In those far-off days petrol cost the equivalent of 20p a gallon, and by the time we reached Delhi the captain (as we called the doctor) calculated he had spent about £100 on it after driving some five to six thousand miles. We took two months to complete the journey since we wanted to do as much sightseeing as possible in Turkey and Iran, and foodwise our life was one great picnic as we had all our meals *al fresco* except when we spent a few nights in great cities like Istanbul, Ankara and Teheran.

The cooking was done on the primus stoves because the captain had been informed that gas cylinders were unobtainable in many places on our route, and that wood was virtually non-existent throughout Turkey and Iran. I well remember meeting two Swiss boys who were travelling to India on a Vespa and had planned to buy food on their way and cook it on bonfires. Since there was no wood lying about in the treeless wilds of Anatolia they were almost starving – they had to fill themselves up in restaurants in the towns they came through and had hardly any money left.

Primus stoves are so fierce that the ideal pot to use on them is a pressure cooker. I used to cook our supper in one every night, so that we could usually eat within an hour of setting up camp. We eventually got rather bored with the mutton we bought in the Turkish bazaars and thought that chicken would be a welcome change. Accordingly when we came to a small town called Nevsehir, crowned by an Ottoman fortress, we tried to make some men understand that we wanted to buy poultry, but they took us to the police station! There we began to flap our arms up and down and cluck loudly, and everyone laughed and understood perfectly what we wanted. We were taken to a large farmyard on the outskirts of the town where a number of scrawny little cockerels and hens were scratching around. With the permission of the farmer (using the language of gesticulation) we caught two. Now having had a poultry farm, I had learnt the quickest and most humane way to kill chickens. I dispatched the pair by dislocating their heads from the necks, handed one to the captain and advised him to pluck it at once while I did the other, as they are so much easier to feather when they are still warm. Disgruntled murmurs immediately arose from the many onlookers who had accompanied us out of the town, and I suddenly realised the reason. I had let no blood, and Muslims as well as Jews insist on this being done, so we quickly paid for the birds, beat a hasty retreat into the Dormobile, and drove off to Urgup, some twelve miles further on, plucking as we went.

We now found ourselves in the most extraordinary landscape in the middle of Cappadocia: for about twenty miles through a valley erosion has left huge cones about a hundred feet high, some of which look like decaying teeth, others like towers, needles and pyramids formed of ashes and rock. These are collectively known as the Rock-cut Monasteries of Cappadocia because, during the seventh and eighth centuries, whole communities of Christians settled in the area and cut out of the rock churches and monasteries which they decorated with wall paintings in the provincial Byzantine style. It was very rewarding to come across many renderings of St George killing his dragon, as he is traditionally believed to have come from this part of Turkey.

We found a wonderful campsite at the head of the valley in a small sandy field with superb views and a large rock wall to one side over which we hung our bedding to dry during the day. We became so enthralled exploring the churches and monasteries and anchorites' cells that we ended up spending three nights there.

But to return to the supper picnic on the evening of our arrival. I decided to prepare a *suprême de volaille* by cooking the elderly, tough little chickens in the pressure cooker, and the rice in an open saucepan on the other stove. After half an hour I wanted to let the pressure down quickly so that I could get on with making the sauce out of the stock. In the centre of a pressure cooker is a weight; when you lift it off it makes a violent hissing sound which always terrifies me, so I asked the captain if he dared do it. He immediately removed not just the weight but the whole lid, whereupon the cooked birds leaped high into the air and disappeared in the inky blackness of a moonless night!

We were all mad with disappointment at being thus deprived of what had promised to be one of the most gastronomically exciting picnics of our journey, but we did not give up hope. For the next twenty minutes we all crawled about on our hands and knees and, with the aid of two very feeble torches, we finally ran them to earth – literally, for they were covered with the dusty grey soil of the region. Undaunted, we plunged them into a bucket of water and, while the girls washed and jointed them, I made a delicious *sauce suprême* with fat, flour, the stock, a little dried milk powder, and the juice of half a small lemon. I did not add the extra refinement of egg yolks as our egg supply was low and we needed them for breakfast.

We finally sat down in a circle round our old hurricane lamp to a scrumptious meal of chicken and rice and sauce and green beans that we had bought in the market at Nevsehir, followed by delicious little white grapes, and all washed down by unadulterated spring water. Water in Turkey is famous for its excellence and the Turks, who are forbidden wine by their religion, talk rapturously of the water of various regions as others would of the wines in France or Italy.

I think our Cappadocian chicken picnic was the best we had on the whole trip, all the more for being so hard won. I was also very proud of the jam roly-poly I made when we were allowed to camp in the harem of Xerxes in Persepolis but that, as Kipling would say, is another story.

Freya Stark

There is quite a streak of adventure running through some of the contributors to this book. I first met the explorer Freya Stark when we were both staying with the Astors at Clivedon. I told her how much she reminded me of one of my ancestors, Jane Digby, whereupon Freya told me that she knew all about Jane whom she saw as a role model. Jane Digby had been born at Holkham at the beginning of the nineteenth century to Admiral Sir Henry Digby and Lady Jane Elizabeth Coke. She had an extraordinary life and was married four times, in relationships which took her to Germany and Greece where for a while she had an affair with the Thessalian general during the Greek War of Independence. She died in Damascus in 1881 after a long and happy marriage to Sheik Medjuel el Mezrab who was twenty years her junior. I think Jane provided a connection between Freya and I, whom I got to know quite well. I visited her once for lunch at her house in Asola in northern Italy. She was quite small and had had a terrible accident when she was young in a factory in Italy when her hair had been caught in a machine, tearing her scalp and ripping her right ear off. As a result she often wore hats to cover her scars or wore her hair draped over to one side. She was wonderful and such an interesting person to have known.

Dartmoor Picnic
Freya Stark

The best picnics I have known were taken during solitary rides about Dartmoor, on the back of one or other of two home-bred, intelligent animals who would stand still in the heather while I got on or off. When we felt hungry, we would find a flat granite stone and I would sit and undo the sandwiches that Cook had prepared, while the black or the bay nuzzled over my shoulder for the lump of sugar that was coming. The moor spread everywhere around, dipping to its rivers, and a quiet happiness blossomed, not only across its brown and healthy spaces, but also from a familiar and beloved atmosphere of countless generations who had felt the same happiness that I was feeling now.

Desmond Doig

Continuing the adventurous profile of some of the contributors was Desmond Doig. A friend of Zanna's, he was something of a Renaissance man: a journalist, artist, photographer and writer, he was the *Statesman*'s roving reporter in Calcutta and is said to have been the first person to write about Mother Theresa. He was also great friends with Edmund Hillary and in 1963 they went together to the Himalayas on an expedition funded by the National Geographic Society to find the abominable snowman. So his wonderful picnic 'When Abominable Snowmen Went Picnicking' was clearly drawn from his own experience!

When Abominable Snowmen Went Picnicking
Desmond Doig

My favourite picnic story comes from Sherpa country below Mount Everest and is about 250 years old. That was the time when the area fairly crawled with yetis – or abominable snowmen.

They became a nuisance, particularly as one of their pastimes was carrying off beautiful young women. In a village called Khumjung, from which some of the most famous Sherpas come, yetis became so thick on the ground that they got in the way. They preyed on precious yaks, dug up valuable potato fields and made the nights alarming with their high-pitched screaming and whistling. Besides, they smelled and were bad-tempered.

The most wise and wily Sherpa elders got together in a series of drunken conferences. How could they rid themselves of the yetis, remembering that they themselves were good Buddhists and couldn't slay the beasts, and that there were some, particularly the lamas, who considered the abominable creatures to be more holy than undesirable.

Unfortunately the person who thought up the prizewinning idea has long since been forgotten. It was, remember, a boozy gathering. The Sherpas of Khumjung, it was decided, would go on one of their popular picnics. Great bowls of potato beer were made by the village ladies, and even more potent bowls of doped *rakshi*, or potato spirit. There were also enough meat dumplings, called *momos*, to build a large house. The curious yetis watched as the villagers, dressed in their brocaded and woolly best, took off to a clearing on a hill nearby and there set to feasting and drinking. Obviously they thought nothing about the fact that every man carried two swords, one made of wood, the other the real thing.

When the Sherpas had had their fill of food and drink, they began to gamble, and then fell to fighting. Wooden swords were drawn and almost every man was 'killed'. Death had never been so noisy and dramatic. Some victims threshed about so much that they almost landed in the river thousands of feet below. Women joined in, torn between lamentation and chopping each other up. The yetis looked on in amazement until it was almost dark. By then the few Sherpas left 'alive' had been dragged by the 'survivors' to their huts. The great pots of doped spirits and hundreds of genuine sharpened swords were left behind. Now it was time for the yetis to have their picnic and, being powerful mimics, it was not long before they feasted and drank, then made a pretence at playing and finally fell upon each other with the swords abandoned by the 'dead' Sherpas.

Great was the slaughter as each side whistled up reinforcements from the dark surrounding mountains, and yetis of all sizes and sexes hurled themselves into the fray. Just a few remained to clear up the battlefield as the Sherpas had done. But when morning came three yeti corpses still remained to be cleared away, and it was on these that the Sherpas descended and removed their scalps as relics to be kept in the village monasteries.

The scalps are still there, in the Sherpa monasteries of Khumjung, Pangboche and Namc Bazar, where they are looked upon with a certain awe and reverence. For years they baffled mountaineers and scientists to whom a few hairs filched from the scalps were sent. The Khumjung scalp became one of the most important clues in the hunt for the elusive snowmen.

In 1960 the mountaineer Sir Edmund Hillary, an eminent American zoologist named Marlin Perkins, and I borrowed the scalp on pain of several very horrid deaths and took it to Chicago, New York, London and Paris. Quite a picnic! It was declared a fake, made from the hide of a wild goat.

Does this mean the epic Sherpa and yeti picnic didn't really happen? It's almost like declaring the Tower of London non-existent if the Crown Jewels turn out to be fakes.

Momos (Tibetan Meat Dumplings)

> 1 oz (25 g) yeast
> 1 cup (250 ml) warm water
> 1 teaspoon sugar
> 1½ lb (700 g) plain flour
> 8 oz (225 g) minced beef
> 1 onion, chopped
> salt
> pepper
> 1 tablespoon olive oil

Dissolve the yeast in a cup of warm water with the sugar. Mix with the flour and knead into a dough. Put in a warm place until the dough rises (about 3–4 hours).

Divide the dough into a dozen portions and, using flour to prevent it sticking, roll each portion into a flat round shape about 3 inches (7.5 cm) in diameter.

Meanwhile mix the minced beef with the chopped onion, seasoning and oil and work it into a stuffing. Take a piece of dough and place a piece of this stuffing in the centre. Turn up the sides of the dough to wrap around the stuffing until only a small opening is left at the top; pinch this opening together. Place all the uncooked dumplings in a hot steamer and steam for about 20 minutes.

Lady Diana Cooper and John Julius Norwich

Lady Diana Cooper had a reputation for being the most beautiful woman in England and was also very clever, all the men were keen on her. She was a distant relative of Colin's, and we thought it was a great coup that she agreed to write about a picnic for us. Like Harold Acton and Dorothy Lygon, she also inspired a character in Evelyn Waugh's work. 'Mrs Stitch' who featured in *Scoop* was a well-connected British socialite who could 'fix' things for people. Diana was at the centre of a group of intellectuals in London and acted in films and on stage before her marriage. When her husband Duff Cooper was made Ambassador to France just after the second world war, the soirées she hosted at the British Embassy turned it into a central hub for post-war French literary culture. She wrote as she talked, which I think you can tell from her picnic, and was an extremely charismatic person. I remember going to see her not long before she died in her lovely house in Little Venice. We were taken up to her bedroom where chairs had been put round her bed, and we all had drinks – she was very keen on drinks – while she reclined in bed wearing a lace nightdress and little cape. We were all paying court and utterly in thrall to her.

I've always known her son John Julius through Diana. He became an historian and made several television and radio programmes. He was very good but I always felt he'd been dealt a very strong hand by being the only son of Diana. His Saharan picnics more than live up to the picnics of the other adventurers in this collection!

Memories of Chantilly
Diana Cooper

I have loved picnics for more than eighty years, ever since a feeder embroidered 'Don't be dainty' in cross-stitch was tied around my baby neck. I still do when I am supported by strong hands to the site, and watch the baskets opened and the unexpected unwrapped. Where once it was hard-boiled egg, dry, curly meat sandwiches and perhaps a banana, eaten anywhere, it is now deliberately a surprise of rareness – iced phantasies, cups of fresh fruits, nameless delicacies, gobbled or sipped in selected venues of sunlight or speckled shade and shine... by the water, on the hilltop, darkly in a tropic wood, or warmed on a rug with mulled wine and ginger against the dangerous beauty of blanketing snow.

In arranging picnics I regard the element of surprise almost as an essential. Classical busts of emperors, in a very wide circle – in the heart of a forest in France, where I once lived – all had to be dressed and elaborately hatted, for instance, and I must be the most astonished of the guests. Surprise forbids attendants, anticipation and talk to announce the diversion. On, towards the middle of a summer's evening, with the customary seven or eight friends munching their chicken, that particular picnic's perpetrator said, 'Listen, you've got to be good about this! No, no, you *must* – my neighbour, Madame de X, a sad widow with a very sick son, begged me to cheer her up by bringing you round for coffee and dessert. I knew you'd all be odious about it but it's ten minutes away and we'll be back within the hour. Please help! No, I can't go alone.'

They followed in fury and found themselves in the early night on an eighteenth-century stone terrace with ice creams, liqueurs – no widow – a couple of young lovers and a half moon. Their relief brought the picnic its high spirits – so there we laughed and sang, out of tune, for two hours.

I think my highwater mark of surprise picnics was one that took place countless years ago, when I was living at Chantilly. Cruising around, I discovered a lake surrounded with statues and a sensible, beautiful boathouse. The nobleman who owned it – unknown to me on solicitation – allowed me a picnic on a Sunday. A few guests were staying at my little château in the Chantilly Park. My four or five weekenders and one millionaire from Paris, all expecting a none-too-good lunch at 1.30, were told that we must see this lovely lake at 12.30 – well worth a slight delay. Sudden panic! A message from an 'agent' told me that M. le Comte would be shooting that morning, but should be shot out by 12.30.

So off we all went at 12.40 through a forest where stood some kind of post round which were laid aperitifs (strong) and usual and unusual scraps. 'Good god!' I cried. 'Look what the Count has left us! What courtesy!' Beneath the speckling sun we quaffed and nibbled and blessed nobility.

This little delight was not two hundred yards from the marvellous lake, and one impatient guest sneaked off for a preview. She returned, panting, having recognised my china and pictures, to tell us with a wink from me that she had seen a lunch for eight in the boathouse, with flowers and fruit and bottles – a surprise indeed! And there we feasted, before my total exhaustion.

I have witnessed and delighted in official picnics – and one especially I can never forget, though it was the opposite of surprise. It was with Winston Churchill, no less, in Marrakesh in 1944. The site was chosen with meticulous care, on the brink of a baby canyon chosen at African dawn after two hours' search by Lady Churchill and a daughter and me – a dramatic scenario with a steep footpath through rocks and hazards of all kinds.

The 'start' was at midday and consisted of quite a procession – a food waggon, two or three chairs, linen, rugs, and implements of all sorts in another van, which included a sprinkling of police and detectives. These were followed by four or five picnickers' cars, including (to enliven my heart) Lord Beaverbrook – beloved assistant of the Prime Minister's court – and quite a few young people like flowers, gathered from I knew not where. On arrival at one o'clock the tables were laid, the rugs spread and chairs arranged – I think for the PM, Lord Beaverbrook, and Lord Moran, the great doctor, always in devoted yet mute attendance.

During this planning the young and middle-aged (myself included) took a spirited rash dash down the craggy path to look nearer the rapid, foaming little river and its huge boulders. The young men were soon half-nude and splashing hardily and scrambling none too nimbly over massive rocks. Proudly we swarmed up that fearful path again to a welcome of drinks and appreciation of our description of the dangers we had passed.

The meal, as always, because of its rarity and difference, passed hilariously, with plenty of elderly wit and youthful zest, ending with coffee, dates and brandy galore. 'Lord Moran thinks I should have another glass of brandy.' Several times Lord Moran's unspoken orders were obeyed and I realised suddenly what was inevitable

– namely Winston's resolve to go down the canyon's perilous path. No word of protest either from Lord Moran or from the great man's wife! The young were not perturbed. I was properly alarmed and stood breathless with the elders halfway down to watch, thank god, his safe descent, supported by police and detectives.

At the bottom, where the young and tipsy started trying to scale again with greater enthusiasm these smooth boulders, Winston Churchill must try too and, what's more, with the dragging and pushing of strong detectives, he succeeded in sprawling successfully to the top of them. Watching, I could think only of his steep return, of his fatigue, of his dear heart. I thought of his being dragged up by his arms so soon after lunch. 'A rope, a rope!' If only I could get one round the Prime Minister's middle so he could be pulled up smoothly. No good, no rope. All I could find was a very long and narrow white tablecloth. It would have to do. I seized it and tore down the perilous path. Anxiety shod my feet with sureness, and success crowned the effort. The dear man revelled in the relief of laying his weight upon the offered support, and reached the top daisy-fresh.

I think I have said enough about picnics, delectable as they always must be, unless sodden with rain and wind on a birdless grouse moor. The *change* is the magic. The hungry nomad surely gets no thrill – poor nomad!

Sahara Picnics
John Julius Norwich

I love picnics; indeed, I once had 147 of them running. That was in 1966, when I spent seven weeks crossing and recrossing the Sahara. As far as I remember I enjoyed them all – all, at least, except two, because they had to be eaten during a sandstorm, and the sand always managed to get into one's mouth before anything else did.

There were seven of us, in the capable hands of a first-class *Saharien* guide, Jean Sudriez, who knew better than anyone the secrets of successful desert catering. These include one great fundamental truth: that the food provided for expeditions like ours should be not only nourishing but, within the limits imposed by the circumstances, good. The Sahara demands austerities enough, and there is no point in adding to them unnecessarily. He had accordingly scoured the épiceries of Algiers, and loaded one of our three Land Rovers to overflowing with as wide a variety of tinned delicacies as they were able to produce – to be supplemented, of course, by bread, dates and occasional supplies of other fruit and vegetables from the oases along our way.

The breakfast menu was determined by the need to get the blood circulating again after the almost indescribable cold of the desert night – for the air has no moisture in it to retain the heat, and the thermometer plummets after sunset. We would wake up frozen to the marrow, to be revived (as soon as we had got the fire going) by bowls of steaming porridge, washed down by Nescafé or, more often, a delicious Ovaltine-like drink called Banania, which I vaguely remembered having seen advertised, but had never drunk before and have never tasted since. Bread was a rarity; but we had *biscottes*, Ryvita, tinned butter and industrial quantities of jam.

That would be at about six in the morning; lunch, however, was a more moveable feast, for by nine the sun was literally searing off every inch of skin left unprotected and we would simply stop wherever some unusual feature of the landscape offered the chance of a bit of shade. At high noon, such blessings are rare. The sun blazes down from immediately above one's head and, in the absence of any trees outside an oasis, the best that can usually be hoped for is some little outcrop of rock with a few overhangs beneath which to huddle.

Sometimes we would stretch an awning between two Land Rovers; but the Sahara is a windy place and the operation was seldom as easy as it sounds. Once settled, we would dig into the usual picnic fare – pilchards and pâté, liverwurst and cheese; but the real pleasure came afterwards, with the cool and sloshy – the tinned asparagus, the peperoni and fruit salad that slip down parched throats like a benediction, caressing and refreshing as they go. No wine at lunchtime; in such heat it would have destroyed us, and we didn't even want it. But the water was wonderful because, thanks to our *guerbas*, it was always cold.

The *guerba* is a wonderful thing. A swollen, still furry and all too recognisable carcass of a goat may not be the most attractive of containers for one's drinking water, but its porousness permits just the right degree of evaporation to keep the contents cool, and its position on the outside of the car gives it the full benefit of the breeze. It hangs upside down, by what used to be the legs; a small plug, inevitably if somewhat indelicately placed at one end, serves as a tap. Cold running water in the Sahara noonday, whatever its taste, colour or provenance, is a commodity not to be despised. We each drank well over a gallon a day.

By nightfall it would be cold again, and there would be a new edge to the wind. The fire would be lit – we never missed the occasional opportunity to stock up with firewood or dried bracken, any more than we did with water – and a few more of our precious tins would be emptied into the pot: spaghetti perhaps, or lentils, or chilli con carne as the *pièce de résistance*, with the usual concomitants of sausage, tuna fish and cheese, rounded off with a few succulent spoonfuls of condensed milk flavoured with caramel or Grand Marnier and washed down with *vin rosé*. Those dinners were for me one of the high spots of the day. We would go on sitting round the fire for as long as it lasted, then put on every available sweater, zip ourselves into first our woollen tracksuits and then our sleeping bags, and sleep under the stars till it was time for breakfast again.

Such was the basic regime on which we covered some eight hundred miles of desert; and even when we found ourselves in the Tibesti Mountains and had to abandon our Land Rovers for camels it did not change appreciably; the only difference was that camel milk suddenly became available as an optional extra. For two or three days after stopping in an oasis we might supplement it with fresh bread, lettuce and tomatoes, and once we were able to buy a whole *guerba* stuffed full of date paste – which, scooped out with the fingers and carried straight to the mouth, was one of the memorable gastronomic pleasures of my life. But these were bonuses. Tins were the staple, and it is hard to see how we could possibly have improved on them. There was only one serious misfortune that we were called upon to suffer: the *vin rosé* ran out after five and a half weeks. But by then, hardened *Sahariens* that we were, we had learned to take disaster in our stride.

Washing up was never a problem. Though water was naturally far too precious to waste on such a purpose, the desert did every bit as well. One dug the plate or fork or mug into the sand, scoured it round for a moment, and the job was done as well as in any kitchen sink. The sand also solved the problem of what to do with the rubbish. We buried it carefully about a foot deep, then carefully smoothed over the place until there was no sign left of where it had been. This sort of habit is every bit as important in the deep Sahara as anywhere else – perhaps even more so, since in that dryness nothing ever decays. Once outside the oases, the desert is the cleanest place in the world; and it is also, to me at least, one of the most beautiful. It has a sparkling purity about it unlike anywhere else I have been; one longs for it to remain like that for ever.

Nicky Haslam

I've known Nicky for most of my life. We have a lovely holiday once a year with this great friend of ours who is Turkish and has a huge yacht. Nicky and I are much the oldest of the group and what we like to do is cruise until we get to a lovely beach with sunloungers and hopefully an ice-cream kiosk. Everyone else goes off being desperately active, diving and whizzing about on jet skis whilst Nicky and I like sitting with our ice creams and watching the world go by. He was also a friend of Diana Cooper's and was always at all the parties. He knew lots of film stars and was always throwing wonderful parties for them whenever they were in London. I particularly remember a very glamorous evening he organised for the French actress Leslie Caron – he always ensured that every little detail was perfect.

The party he describes, a birthday picnic he organised for Diana Cooper is typical of the gorgeous evenings he would create for his friends, and fits Diana's own essential picnic criteria by including an element of surprise.

Some Enchanted Evening
Nicky Haslam

Summer, many years ago, in Venice. A light zephyr cooled the tiles and terraces; the roses and jasmine trembled, the gondolas nuzzled each other's prows on the narrow canal, the water on the lagoon beyond stood still as mirror glass. It was cocktail hour, and it was Diana Cooper's birthday.

'Let's,' I said, 'take the boats and drinks and drift gently among those deserted little islands for an hour or so.'

'Oh, yes, do let's,' said one of the many guests, Minnie Astor, maybe, or Dick Avedon, 'there's masses of time before dinner.'

Within minutes we were settled on cushions, the *remi* silently moving us across the sunset-splashed surface. Dusk came fast, sky and water became one. The two boats echoed with laughter; glasses were refilled; our cigarettes' glow reflected in ripples around us, gradually augmented by first stars and then, in golden fragments, the tiara of lights along the distant Adriatic shoreline.

Now night fell.

'Shouldn't we turn back soon?'

'Suppose so, but maybe just a few minutes more... '

Then: 'What's that sound? Music?' asked Simon Fleet.

'Yes, over there.'

'No, *there,* from *that* island.'

'Surely there's only a ruined lighthouse on it?'

'But I think there are lights as well. Perhaps it's a party,' said Diana. 'Let's look.'

The boats turned; we drew nearer, the music louder now, the light flickering on tumbled arches hung with garlands of zinnias. Diana was the first ashore. She called to us, amazed. 'Quick! Come!'

We scrambled from the boats. And saw the table swagged with green, the candles amid branches, ice-cold wine and pitchers of Diana's favourite – vodka and grapefruit. We heard the musicians playing a soft bacarolle, while our two houseboys produced baskets of toasted ham and cheese sandwiches, figs with proscuitto, peaches and other Venetian delights that young Arrigo Cipriani had secretly sent across from Harry's Bar a few hours earlier.

With the help of the boys I'd found the island, and we'd spent the day creating this bucolic mise en scène; its ambiance became more enchanting each midnight moment. In fact, until the stars faded. And it being Diana's birthday we sang. And danced.

Colette Clark

A friend who had a famous father and went on to have a famous son was Colette Clark. She was the daughter of the art historian and broadcaster Kenneth Clark, presenter of the series *Civilisation* on the BBC in the 1960s. She was very direct, called a spade a spade and used to have fantastic dinner parties. She brought up her son Sam on her own and he was at school with my son Christopher. He went on to open the successful Moro restaurants with his wife who is also called Sam. I've read that he remembered his mother's glamorous dinner parties and realised what joy and fun food could bring to people. It's rather nice to think that I might have been at one of the dinner parties that inspired such a talented and successful chef.

A Picnic in Portugal
Colette Clark

The best food I have eaten on a picnic was cooked by a farmer's wife in a tiny village in northern Portugal. My brother had asked her for something to take with us on a walk up the foothills of the Minho mountains in search of a series of waterfalls, and this is what she provided: two freshly cooked marinated chickens from her own farmyard; slices of cold veal coated in a spicy glacé sauce; meat and egg croquettes (*croquetas*) which were still warm but of such perfect consistency – firm but light – that they could be eaten with the fingers. To this were added home-made bread rolls, tomatoes and fruit from her garden and, to crown it all, little cold pancakes filled with cherry jam and dusted with cinnamon. But it is the croquettes I will remember.

Egg Croquettes

> 1½ oz (40 g) butter
> 1½ oz (40 g) flour
> 8 fl. oz (200 ml) milk flavoured with salt, pepper and bayleaf
> 4 hard-boiled eggs
> 2 raw egg yolks
> parsley, chopped
> pinch of nutmeg
> salt
> fresh white breadcrumbs
> oil and butter for frying

Make a sauce by melting the butter, adding the flour, and cooking to make the roux. Add the milk gradually, stirring all the time. Cook for 5 minutes, then leave to cool a little. Add the chopped eggs, one egg yolk, parsley and nutmeg. Leave on a plate to get cold (it is best to prepare up to this point the night before, or several hours in advance if that is not possible).

Roll into fat sausage shapes on a board covered in seasoned flour, then dip into the beaten yolk of an egg to which you have also added salt. Then roll in a large quantity of fresh white breadcrumbs and fry in a mixture of very hot oil and butter until golden brown (a basket which can be lowered into the fat makes this easier). Drain on kitchen paper one by one, and leave to cool for the picnic.

Meat Croquettes

> 12 oz (350 g) cooked veal or beef
> 1 onion
> ½ oz (10 g) butter
> a small bunch of parsley, chopped
> ½ pint (250 ml) good gravy
> salt and pepper
> 1 beaten egg
> breadcrumbs

Mince the meat in a food processor for just a second or two. Chop the onion and soften in the butter in a frying pan. Add the meat, parsley, gravy, salt and pepper. The consistency should be moist, but firm enough to shape into croquettes once it has cooled down. Then proceed as for egg croquettes.

Christopher Thynne

Christopher was the second son of the 6th Marquess of Bath, the owner of Longleat. He was the Comptroller of Longleat up until his older brother, Alexander, inherited the title in 1993, at which point he was sacked and thrown off the estate. His relationship with Alexander, who was known for having lots of mistresses he called 'Wifelets' wasn't easy, I think having to find cottages on the estate for all these wifelets could be tricky. At one point Christopher thought he was going to have to have one of them living with him but then an alternative was found. When we went to visit Christopher he wasn't getting on with his brother so we only saw the safari park, we didn't go into the house. It was a shame as I was dying to see the famous murals of the Karma Sutra which had been painted inside! Christopher was great fun and loved writing limericks so I wasn't surprised when he wrote us a poem for his picnic.

Anne Glenconner

The Longleat Picnic
Christopher Thynne

Sun is sinking, cars are loaded
Children, food and frying pans,
A basket full of drink and tumblers,
Lemonade and Cola cans.

Dogs are barking, parents shouting,
Dressed in jeans and tweedy suits,
'Have we got a bottle opener?
Sophie, you've forgot your boots.'

The cavalcade of cars starts rolling,
Someone shouts, 'Who's got the pugs?'
Silvy runs back from the Mill House
Loaded with a pile of rugs.

Start again, out through the driveway,
Swirling dust clouds in our wake,
Down the lane and through the woodland,
Heading for the Island Lake.

I love the sound and smell of cooking,
Everybody's had a drink,
One or two are on their second,
Ed is on his third, I think.

Christopher Thynne

Alexander's acting strangely,
Think he's getting rather tight.
Now he's dancing like a dervish,
Someone's set his beard alight.

Tony's chatting up the Duchess.
I think he sometimes goes too far.
The fire's burning rather well now,
Think I'll strum on my guitar.

I'm sure I put it here beside me.
Now it's vanished from my sight.
Oh my god – some stupid bugger,
So that's why the fire's so bright.

Christ! It's getting rather cold now,
Wish that I was in my car,
Put my coat on, pick up litter,
Throw some wood on my guitar.

Time to go now – what a pity,
Just as things were going well,
Life's a picnic – earth's a heaven,
Both to me just now are hell.

Grope our way back through the darkness,
Tree Trunk Bridge I see, I think.
What's that splash? Dad's in the water –
That's goodbye to all the drink.

Matches flare and fade like fireflies,
Someone's fallen in the stream,
Voices calling all around me,
Havoc's reigning quite supreme.

What the hell? – I think I'll stay here,
Wrap up warm – I'll be all right,
I'd only fall into the water –
We're coming back tomorrow night.

Derek Hill

Visiting Derek Hill at his cottage in Ireland was a somewhat terrifying experience. He had bought us plane tickets to Belfast rather than Dublin and, on the way, the taxi ran into a confrontation on the Shankhill Road. The driver made us all lie down in the back of the car to avoid the shooting. We were petrified. But Derek was totally unsympathetic when we eventually arrived at his house. I suppose it was a pretty run-of-the-mill experience for him. He was a painter, Director of Fine Arts at the British School in Rome and a great friend of King Charles. He used to accompany the King on some of his trips abroad to be on hand to advise him as he painted. The King is an excellent artist; he paints beautiful watercolours. Derek did the portraits of various members of the Royal Family, but he also painted a portrait of me which I love.

A Painter's Picnic
Derek Hill

Thinking back over picnics is, I find, no strain to my memory: the landscape, to a painter, is as important as the meal itself. I remember picnics in all sorts of places: in pinewoods in Bavaria, dashing down to a nearby lake to bathe with my cousins while my mother and Aunt Lucy watched, trying to photograph our splashings with trembling hands and shaky results. Then, a few years later when I was a student, picnics in France during painting excursions under those exquisite Ile de France skies of floating clouds and Impressionist river scenes; rarely attended by French friends, who, when they did overcome their dislike of informality and the deep countryside, insisted on correct placement and table linen.

In post-war years there was a vividly remembered picnic in Turkey at a Hittite site – an ambassadorial picnic with the chief archaeological experts in the country as our guides. A liveried chauffeur helped with the 'furniture' and the 'site' – custodians stood at a respectful distance watching the unusual scene. We had a delectable cold Turkish soup called *Leyla* that I was greedy enough to get the recipe for.

Sandwiches, in spite of my grandmother having made a dictionary of them in her handwritten book of recipes, are the one thing that I can do without at any meal, unless they are of the delicious and thinly cut cucumber variety that used to be offered at tennis-party teas. Nowadays they are never thin enough, and the cucumber is seldom peeled. But back to my grandmother: she listed sandwiches of chopped figs and lemon cream, dates, bananas, herring with mustard sauce, olives chopped with ham and cheese, sardines and watercress – an infinite and mouth-watering variety. Today the bread always seems too heavy for the filling, and after one mouthful one feels 'full up to dollies' wax', as Nanny used to call one's bloated state.

If you live, as I do, in one of the wettest climates in the British Isles (Donegal) something warm is needed, and something that can be eaten in a shelter or a neighbour's porch, should the wind and rain be too extreme. It is a rule here never to cancel a picnic because of the weather, which can change completely within a matter of hours. A large thermos filled with risotto or kedgeree is popular, and then a salad packed into a big apple-shaped ice bucket that keeps it cool and fresh; cheese and a tin of Bath Oliver biscuits and slices of almond cake in foil. I am fortunate enough to own a Sardinian wicker basket, which kind Italian friends bought me as a house present; it is 'upholstered' inside with all possible picnic requirements and large enough to hold a banquet.

This picnic essay started about landscape as an ingredient essential to a painter's pleasure, but a more culinary and basic interest has inevitably intervened. Perhaps Bernard Berenson was right when he used to say, 'The trouble with Derek is that he never paints between meals.' I know that even on a perfect day in the most beautiful surroundings, I often regret that my Sardinian basket isn't stocked with paints and brushes rather than the splendid provisions packed by Gracie, my housekeeper.

Leyla Soup (for four)

- 1 tablespoon butter
- 1 heaped dessertspoon flour
- 2 pints (1 litre 150 ml) chicken stock
- 2 eggs

1½ lemons
freshly chopped mint
2 tablespoons tomato juice
salt and pepper
1 pint (570 ml) yoghurt

Melt the butter and slightly cook the flour in it. Add the stock slowly. Bring to the boil, stirring all the time. Beat the eggs till they froth, add the strained juice of the lemons, and stir into the stock (having first added a few tablespoons of the stock to the egg and lemon) very slowly. Add some chopped mint and the tomato juice. Season with salt and pepper. Bring to the boil again. Add the yoghurt but do not reboil.

Ian Graham

When I came out as a debutante in London in 1950 Ian Graham was a dancing partner of mine. He was keen on vintage cars and used to come and pick me up wearing goggles and a flying jacket. I was quite shy and felt terribly embarrassed to be seen in these cars, which ruined your hairdo. In those days we all had rather neat hairstyles which got blown to smithereens, despite the scarf you would be handed rather crossly when you got in. He fell out of my life and disappeared from the London scene. In fact, he drove a vintage Rolls Royce across America and down to Mexico where he first came across Mayan sculpture, which became his passion and job. He became an eminent Mayanist, involved with preserving and cataloguing ruins. He spent so much time working in Central America it's entirely appropriate his picnic recalls al fresco eating in Guatemala.

Picnic in Guatemala
Ian Graham

On hearing that I take all my meals out of doors during several months of the year, and that I generally eat them sitting on the ground in a forest, you might suppose me to be either mad, or a keen and expert picnicker. Alas, as a picnicker I am neither keen nor expert. My apparent mania for al fresco dining is no more than a consequence of the kind of archaeological work I undertake in Guatemala, and the meals that I provide are decidedly not good picnic fare. Far from being fresh and appetising in appearance, or made up with a due proportion of vegetables and fruit into unusual, perhaps even surprising dishes, mine are nearly always stodgy affairs in which rice, black beans and tortillas routinely play the leading roles, and they are mostly devoured in a perfunctory way during respites from work. Unfortunately, fruit and vegetables soon rot in the tropical heat, and before an expedition is two weeks old they have disappeared from the menu.

Even a French explorer seems to have despaired of the available materials. In describing a journey through these same regions a century ago, Désiré Charnay gives a menu: it starts with *Soupe d'haricots noirs* and goes on predictably to *Haricots noirs rissolés*, but his *vin de Bordeaux* must have made the meal more bearable. Evidently his mule train clanked along to the music of wine bottles, one of which I even found, still unbroken, near a waterhole by which he must have camped. I imagine that in spite of the poor provender, strict etiquette was observed, even in that sweltering jungle; a photograph shows his secretary properly dressed in a frock coat.

Still, I *have* sometimes tried to provide a picnic worthy of the name for a visitor, particularly one who has brought in fresh supplies. And in the absence of such supplies there is always a chance of finding crunch, one of the most delicious being heart of palm. But to obtain something growing in the forest that will contribute freshness, one has to find a tree at just the right stage of growth, and fell it with an axe.

Of these more ambitious picnics, some may be counted successful. At least none has been more unsuccessful as the one mentioned so laconically in *Lolita*. Humbert Humbert, you may remember, tells us that his 'very photogenic mother died in a freak accident (picnic, lightning)'. Nor have any of us yet been struck down by ptomaine poisoning. In this connection, though, I do offer a word of caution that is as relevant to picnics on hot days in temperate climates as it is to the tropics: avoid making up sandwiches or other food with mayonnaise or soft cheese, both of which suit the taste of bacteria all too well. On the other hand, dressings made acid with vinegar or lemon juice put them off.

One picnic I remember, which was nearly ruined by a small mishap, was held in a ruined city of the ancient Maya called La Pasadita, a very small settlement consisting of only a few public buildings perched on a steep hill with vertical rock faces on two sides. Only one building remains standing, and even this seemed doomed to collapse at any moment. Until some fifteen years ago the doorways were spanned by beautifully carved stone lintels, then these were wrenched out by looters. Inside, the walls show the remains of fresco painting, with portraits of rulers and scenes of ceremony. The main elements of our not very sumptuous picnic were: black bean and chorizo salad, empanadas, flour tortillas, mangoes and lemonade.

Black Bean and Chorizo Salad

>8 oz (225 g) black beans or (much better) lentils
>1¾ pints (1 litre) water
>chorizo or other spicy sausage
>1 large onion
>black olives
>1 teaspoon salt
>olive oil
>wine vinegar
>French mustard

Wash the beans or lentils, add them to the water and bring to the boil and cook, but do not allow them to become mushy. Drain. Cut the sausage into cubes, add chopped onion, chopped black olives and salt and blend with the lentils. Before serving, pour over a dressing of olive oil, vinegar and French mustard.

Empanadas

>(Makes about 15)

Pastry

>12 oz (350 g) self-raising flour
>½ teaspoon salt
>4 oz (110 g) butter
>1 egg yolk
>2 tablespoons milk for glaze

Filling

- 1 lb (450 g) minced beef, or pork and beef (wild boar when I made them at La Pasadita)
- 1 tablespoon olive oil
- 1 small onion, chopped
- 1 clove garlic, crushed
- 1 tomato, peeled and chopped
- 2 tablespoons chopped blanched almonds
- ½ teaspoon chilli powder
- 6 dessertspoons raisins
- 6 green olives, pitted and sliced
- 2 teaspoons capers

Put the flour and salt in a bowl. Cut in the butter until thoroughly mixed. Gradually add enough iced water to form a dough. Wrap the dough in plastic film and keep in the refrigerator while you make the filling.

Heat the oil in frying pan and cook the meat until no longer pink, stirring the while. Add onion, garlic, tomato, almonds, chilli powder, raisins (previously soaked in hot water if hard), olives and capers. Cook over reduced heat for 6–8 minutes, stirring frequently. Add salt to taste. If the mixture is still wet, cook longer. Cool.

Preheat the oven to gas mark 5 (375°F, 190°C). Roll out the dough on a floured surface to rather less than 3 mm thick. Cut in squares of about 4 inches (10 cm). Place a tablespoon of the filling in each square, then fold over on the diagonal, and crimp the edges together with your fingertips. Place the empanadas on greased baking tins and brush with a glaze prepared by beating the egg yolk with the milk. Bake for 15–20 minutes until golden. Place on a rack to cool.

Lemonade

A subtly different flavour can be imparted to lemonade by boiling up the lemon peel in it.

Postscript

As it turned out we were not to enjoy the empanadas, so laboriously baked in an improvised oven in our camp near La Pasadita. I left them during the morning hung in a plastic bag on a tree, out of reach of ants; but some animal, probably a large member of the stoat family, enjoyed them instead. So we had to make do with sardines.

Patrick Lindsay

Another friend who had a passion for vintage cars was Patrick Lindsay. He married my cousin Annabel Yorke and I remember Colin and I went to their wedding on the day we announced our engagement. There were lots of press photographers there, but they were all taking photographs of us rather than the couple getting married, Annabel told me later she was furious about that! Patrick was a director at Christie's auction house and loved racing vintage cars. He'd been at Eton and Zanna and I thought it would be rather fun to ask him to write about a Fourth of June Picnic, which is such an institution at the school. It's a day which was originally to commemorate the birthday of King George III but is now just a broader celebration of the school's history. When my son Henry was there I'd call up other mothers and we would arrange to have a picnic in the grounds whilst the cricket match was going on in the background. It was rather an odd sight, especially with all the boys in their stiff winged collars.

Anne Glenconner

Fourth of June Picnic
Patrick Lindsay

Agars Plough. Eton. Fourth of June 1946.
Celebrating King George III's birthday.

The Chairman and the Director of the National Gallery entertain some of their children to a picnic luncheon. Their wives sit on the running board of the exotic V12 cylinder Lagonda Open Tourer.

In the background the soothing snick of leather on willow – the Eton eleven playing their annual cricket match against the Ramblers. Peace – and peacetime at last!

It had been a poor summer. Home-grown strawberries had not been up to scratch. Ours were flown from Israel. Cream obtained with a struggle. My first ever *Pâté en croûte*.

Pâté en Croûte

Dough

    1½ lb (700 g) flour
    1 teaspoon salt
    4 oz (110 g) lard
    4 oz (110 g) butter
    1 egg
    ½ cup cold water

Pâté

    8 oz (225 g) veal
    8 oz (225 g) lean pork

8 oz (225 g) fat pork
2 eggs
salt and pepper
1 tin truffles (optional)
2 tablespoons cognac
12 oz (350 g) lean ham
12 oz (350 g) tongue
dorure (1 tablespoons milk beaten with 1 egg)
aspic
parsley

Mix together the dough ingredients and wrap in waxed paper. Store overnight in the refrigerator.

Line a springform loaf tin with the dough, saving some for later, and bake at gas mark 7 (425°F, 220°C) for 10 minutes. Then remove, and reduce the heat to gas mark 6 (400°F, 200°C). Mince together the veal, lean pork and fat pork. Add 2 eggs, mix well, and pound to a smooth paste. Add salt and pepper. Ignite 2 tablespoons of warmed cognac and stir in. Press the forcemeat through a sieve or purée it in a blender. Cut the ham and tongue into sticks or batons about 1 inch (2.5 cm) thick and as long as possible. Cut the contents of a can of truffles into smaller sticks.

Cover the bottom of the loaf tin with a layer of forcemeat. Arrange parallel rows of truffle and ham a tongue sticks down the length of the tin. Cover these with a layer of forcemeat and proceed in this fashion until full, arranging pink and black batons to make a cross-section pattern when the pâté is sliced. Cover with a thin layer of larding pork and with the remaining dough. Decorate the crust and make a small hole in the centre of the covering to allow steam to escape.

Bake the pâté for about 1½ hours, brushing it once or twice

with *dorure* (mix 1 tablespoon milk with beaten egg) and covering it with heavy buttered paper if it browns too quickly. Cool in the tin. Pour cool but liquid aspic through the hole in the crust to fill spaces created by shrinking during cooking. Chill the pâté well. Garnish with aspic cut-outs and ribbons of finely minced parsley and aspic, stirred to fragments with a fork.

Min Hogg

Colin was utterly thrilled when Min Hogg, who was founding editor of *World of Interiors*, came to the White House, which we had built in Tite Street in 1968, and wrote a very complimentary article about it for the magazine. We had lots of interest in the house which at the time was described as the most stylish in London. There were all sorts of funny stories about Min Hogg – rumours that she had had an affair with the film director John Huston, that she'd refused to sleep with Lucien Freud and that she had held up a very drunk Mick Jagger as they tried to dance together. I have no idea whether any of these were actually true but I do remember her as being very good fun at dinner parties, full of interesting anecdotes and stories. After my worry about choosing mushrooms in Italy I particularly love the first line of her picnic.

Anne Glenconner

Autumn Mushroom Picnic
Min Hogg

If you cannot tell the difference between edible types of wild mushroom and their dangerously poisonous counterparts, this picnic plan could be the most effective way of pruning your circle of friends since dinner at the Borgias. All the same, if you cannot distinguish between them you are missing one of the most delicious of gastronomic treats. I urge you from the bottom of my heart to rectify the situation. Just check on the cost of wild mushrooms in the shops, should you be lucky enough to know of a greengrocer with the enterprise to sell them. It will be enough to convince the profoundest sceptic that they must not only be a delicacy worth trying, but also be worth the price of a guidebook on mushrooms and fungi in order to learn how to obtain the treat for free. There are masses of guides to wild mushrooms in bookshops, and one I find particularly easy to use is called *British and European Mushrooms and Fungi*, published by Chatto and Windus. It is cheap, pocket-size, and every photograph is in colour. The mixture of stern warnings and bubbling enthusiasm in its text seems like a good balance, and it certainly gave me the confidence right from the start to identify and eat what I had picked.

One pale blue morning in mid-October I gathered a basket of mixed mushrooms. They came from a Hampshire woodland spot I know, within sight and sound of the M3. You would be amazed how many rich clusters of fungi are to be found in woods close beside motorways.

Since so many lethal-looking toadstools are, in fact, edible, it is vital to educate yourself about those that have the best taste. There are lots that are either insipid or repulsively slimy, and I have never generated much enthusiasm amongst my guests for anything blue – these are the sort to leave gracing the paths and glades in which they grow. Beginners in toadstool eating should really confine themselves to the Cep and Boletus families; they are delicious and abundant and have the distinguishing feature of something looking like fine sponge rubber on their undersides in place of the gills found in ordinary shop-bought mushrooms. Incidentally, I advise scraping off this benign but slippery sponge stuff before cooking, rather in the way you remove the hairy bit attached to artichoke hearts. Apart from the guidebook, essential at all times, pickers should arm themselves with a knife to slice off the mushroom caps; wrenching the whole stem out of the ground stops other mushrooms from coming up in the same place.

While I was foraging for this picnic my guests were working like Trojans, collecting wood and building a really good fire at our chosen site beside a lake. We balanced over the fire a metal trivet large enough to take two pans: one pan for water – which I had brought as hot as possible in giant thermoses – and the other for the mushrooms. Since the fungi taste extremely rich I decided to cook them as they often do in Italy, sliced and sautéed with parsley and garlic to flavour a simple pasta. As we waited for the spaghetti water to boil I sliced the mushrooms, mixed them with the chopped parsley and crushed garlic, and fried them gently in a little butter. The best spaghetti for picnics is vermicelli. I like its thin gauge which has the inestimable advantage of cooking quickly – even on an open fire.

The minute the pasta was *al dente* and drained, I tipped the mushrooms together with the pan juices on top of it, mixed them all together, and dished them up as quickly as possible.

Nicholas Coleridge

I met Nicholas a few times, although he was mainly a friend of Zanna's. He was always highly entertaining and, of course, became the absolute king of the magazine world, and we all devoured magazines.

Picnic at the Grange
Nicholas Coleridge

I don't know of a more perfect setting for a picnic than the ruins of Grange Park. This is the astonishing Greek Revival house near Micheldever in Hampshire that C.R. Cockerell built for the Baring family, and around which there was so much controversy a few years ago when plans were made to knock it down. Now the shell of the house stands, like the ruins of Priene, at the head of a valley surrounded by cornfields with distant views of a lake beyond.

It is such a dramatic setting that any picnic staged there is a colossal leap upmarket. Even half-a-dozen bread rolls and a slice of veal and ham pie looks rather good eaten underneath the portico of the ballroom, which is the best place to set up a picnic table. All around the ruin are clumps of nettles and dock leaves which conceal quite large fragments of frieze and, if you are very lucky, pieces of broken sculpture. It is rather like scavenging over the plains of Troy except that no little boys rush up with faked antiquities for sale. Until recently you could have vandalised the Neo-Classical mantelpieces too, some of which were suspended in mid-air between floor-less rooms. We talked about it a lot, but you would have needed a crane. Last time I went, however, they had all disappeared and there were deep gaping holes in the plaster. We presumed that a Fulham antique dealer had made a hit-and-run assault with a van at dead of night.

The only disadvantage of Grange Park is that it is impossible to find. I have picnicked there several times and on each occasion driven for hours in convoy, up and down hill, endlessly three-point-turning, pulling into lay-bys at every summit and agreeing that we *must* be able to see it from here. The lanes around Micheldever all look exactly the same and only every half hour or so, when you pass the railway station for the third time, do you realise that you've been driving in a circle.

The entrance to the house is guarded by a lodge and this you must drive past at great speed. Once past, however, there is little chance of being nabbed for trespassing. Grange Park is now run by the Department of the Environment, who have surrounded it with barbed wire and 'Clear off' type signs but haven't, so far, installed a watchman.

My first Grange Park outing was with friends then at the Courtauld Institute of Art, plus Napier Miles who claims to know that part of Hampshire inside out and was map reading, but really only knows it back to front. Our intended lunch had turned into picnic tea by the time we found the house and suddenly it had become very cold. All I can remember is everybody huddled in tartan car rugs sitting on the roof. Possibly we were singing old pop songs to keep warm (I do hope that we weren't). Then someone suggested having a discotheque, with music from the cassette player in the car. This was driven across the bumpy ground to the front of the ballroom portico, and looked like a Ford Fiesta in a colour magazine advertisement. We bopped ludicrously away to David Bowie and Dolly Parton, the music blaring through the open car door. Only when it was time to go home, however, did we realise the snag. The car battery had gone flat and we had to push.

My other notable picnic there was on the hottest Bank Holiday Monday of 1980. We had only taken an hour to find the gate this time, and two even more idiosyncratic carloads were in convoy.

In the sun Grange Park looks like the Acropolis, despite the scaffolding that the Department of the Environment have put around the ballroom to make it resemble the Pompidou Centre in Paris. We were better prepared this time, with a wind-up gramophone and a far superior picnic. Also more to drink.

Could the drink have been the spur for the preposterous photocall after lunch? This was a quite unforeseen craze for recreating old master paintings for the camera. Draped in the tablecloth and lengths of barbed wire, we cut a swathe through the Renaissance to the Pre-Raphaelites in half a dozen well-chosen frames: Guido Reni's *Ecce Homo*; Poussin's *Christ Expelling the Money-lenders from the Temple*; the *Laocoon*; Burne-Jones's *Virgil and Dante Meeting at the River Styx*.

That is the secret ingredient in a Grange Park picnic – the culture factor. If you know anything at all, however banal, about art or architecture you can depend on an opportunity to show off. Certainly it is the only occasion ever that I can consciously recall utilising my end-of-bin Cambridge History of Art degree.

Larissa Haskell

Larissa was a friend of Zanna's and an eminent Russian art historian of Venetian art who had been a curator of Venetian drawings at the Hermitage Museum in St Petersburg in Russia. She married the art historian Francis Haskell and they lived in Oxford. I remember visiting the Hermitage with Colin years ago when the twins were small and he threw the most dreadful tantrum when the babushkas who guard the galleries prevented him from entering a room he was particularly keen to see. An English-speaking curator was summoned to see what the fuss was about but at that point he'd calmed down and somehow managed to charm his way into the room. I sometimes wonder whether that English-speaking curator may have been Larissa.

Russian Picnic
Larissa Haskell

Russian literature is full of poetical descriptions of food. The jolly noise of pots and pans from the kitchen follows like a musical accompaniment to the idyllic childhood of Ilya Ilyich Oblomov in Goncharov's famous novel. Succulent meals of the rich Volga merchants make a reading of Melinikov-Pechersky's novels unbearable on an empty stomach. The joys of good food are celebrated on many pages of Anton Chekhov's stories, but nowhere as vividly as in *Siren*, where a clerk's lusty dream of a festive dinner drives everyone in the office crazy.

What about picnics? A reader who is looking for a menu is likely to be disappointed here – a furtive kiss in the woods would be easier to find. But the essence of a picnic – the special pleasure of eating on grass among the trees – is nowhere expressed better than in Tolstoy's *Childhood, Boyhood, Youth*.

> When we reached woods, we found the carriage already there, and, beyond all our expectations, a cart, in the midst of which sat the butler. In the shade we beheld a samovar, a cask with a form of ice cream, and some other attractive parcels and baskets. It was impossible to make any mistake: there was to be tea, ice cream and fruits in the open air. At the sight of the cart we manifested an uproarious joy; for it was considered a great treat to drink tea in the woods on the grass, and especially in a place where nobody had ever drunk tea before.
>
> Chapter VII, translated by Isabel F. Hapgood

But if a picnic, seen through the eyes of a child, did not leave other memories than ice cream and fruit, the meal eaten by Natasha Rostov after the hunt in *War and Peace* is surprising both in its length and in its colourful description.

Liquors made from herbs, pickles, mushrooms, hot rye cakes, honey in the comb, foaming honey mead, apples, nuts both fresh and roasted and nuts in honey... Preserves made with honey and others made with sugar, ham and freshly roasted chicken...

Translated by Constance Garnett

A meal which would give many an idea to lovers of health food.

Picnics of course become especially popular with the growth of urban life, which adds a value to nature unpolluted by the presence of human beings, and so picnics have become a necessary part of recreation in present-day Russia both for the family and the courting couple seeking privacy. The favourite food is a shish kebab (called *shashlik*), cooked on charcoal in a hole dug into the earth, washed down by great quantities of vodka. I give here a few recipes which, while they are still popular today, could easily have been found in the picnic baskets of Tolstoy or Chekhov.

Pirojki with Spring Onions and Egg

Dough

　　¼ oz (7 g) fresh yeast
　　1 glass warm milk
　　1 lb (450 g) plain flour
　　1 tablespoon melted butter

Filling

　　1 lb (450 g) spring onions
　　butter
　　2 hard-boiled eggs, chopped

To make the dough, dissolve the yeast in the milk. Mix this liquid with the flour and melted butter and leave in a warm place to double in size (no kneading is required) for about an hour. Preheat the oven to gas mark 6 (400°F, 200°C). When ready, cut the dough into eight portions. Mix all the filling ingredients together. Fill each portion of dough with the mixture, seal and bake for one hour. Pirojki should serve as an accompaniment to the main course, for which I propose the following.

Kurinie Kotleti – Chicken Meatballs

(Serves four)

2 boned chicken breasts
1 slice white bread
milk
1 egg
oil for frying

Mince the chicken breasts. Soak the bread in milk and beaten egg and then mix with the chicken. Roll into little balls and fry in a frying pan in hot oil for 20 minutes. The essential thing is not to let the liquid escape.

Valeria Coke

When we were children Carey and I adored swimming in the fountain at Holkham, it was freezing cold but of course when the water came out of the mouths of the dolphins it was all great fun. Valeria was married to my cousin Eddie who inherited Holkham, and she suggested basing her picnic at the fountain. We all joined in, and sat in the sun with Holkham in the background and the park and the deer and the sound of the fountain, it was just glorious.

A Picnic by the Fountain of Perseus and Andromeda, Holkham, Norfolk
Valeria Coke

We usually take our picnics to the beach, a mile away, but on one hot sunny day that I remember we moved only as far as the fountain. When it plays, the fountain is spectacular; but we turn it on only when the house is open to the public as it works on a very complicated system. A vast amount of water is pumped up seven hundred feet from a well – said to be the deepest in Norfolk – to a reservoir a mile up the hill. The pressure of water from this reservoir is so great that, when the taps are turned on, it provides a magnificent display.

On the occasion that I am recalling it was a perfect summer afternoon, and before lunch the braver children clambered down the steps into the pool to swim and play hide-and-seek behind the spouting dolphins. Our picnic consisted of sorrel soup, local Cromer crab pâté, a simple quiche decorated with samphire from the marsh, and an equally simple but delicious pudding.

Sorrel Soup

> 8 oz (225 g) mixed sorrel and lettuce
> 2 oz (50 g) butter
> 1 pint (500 ml) chicken stock
> salt
> 2 egg yolks
> ½ pint (250 ml) cream
> black pepper
> grated nutmeg

Wash and dry the leaves, removing the stalks. Heat the butter in a heavy pan, add the sorrel and lettuce and cook gently for 3 minutes. Heat the stock and pour on. Bring to simmering point, add a little salt and cover the pan. Simmer for 5 minutes. Put in a liquidiser or through a mouli and return to pan. Beat the egg yolks with the cream, stir in one ladleful of hot soup and add to the pan. Add the black pepper and nutmeg to taste. Reheat but do not boil. Serve hot or cold.

Crab Pâté

> 1 clove garlic, crushed
> 1 dessertspoon curry powder
> cayenne
> 2–3 tablespoons mayonnaise
> 1 lb (450 g) crab meat
> melted butter

Add the garlic, curry powder and cayenne to the mayonnaise, and mix with the crab meat to a firm consistency. Press down in an earthenware pot or soufflé dish. Pour on melted butter to seal. Serve with toast or fresh bread and salad.

Raspberries and White Currants in Soured Cream

Mix raspberries and topped and tailed white currants together, dredge with caster sugar, and lightly fold in soured cream.

Sylvia Combe

Aunt Sylvia was always entertaining people, if you turned up at her house the table would be laid for tea in the drawing room, for lunch in the dining room, for supper in the kitchen and for breakfast in the summer house – everything would be ready for whatever might happen. I remember her telling a story about the end of one Christmas after her children had left and she had thought it was the end of the celebrations, so she took the remains of the turkey and tied it up in a tree outside for the birds, she was very keen on birds. Later that morning she heard a car coming up the drive and suddenly remembered she'd invited the Haineses to lunch so she rushed outside, took down the turkey, gave it a quick wash and that's what they had to eat, none the wiser!

She wasn't brought up at Holkham but when the blitz started she was living in London and she wrote to her grandfather to ask if it would be possible for her to bring the children up to Norfolk because London was becoming quite dangerous. He wrote back and said he was afraid it just wouldn't be possible because the nursery footman had been called up and so wasn't available. In reality she could have taken the whole of one wing and no one would have known but the lack of a nursery footman rendered the whole thing impossible, that's just how things were then. She married Simon Combe of Watney, Combe and Reid brewers and Simon's sister married Lord Londonderry. Their daughter was Jane van Tempest Stuart who was my age and also one of the other maids of honour at the Coronation.

We were all sent up to Scotland during the war to stay with my aunt who was the Countess of Airlie. Aunt Sylvia, having not been able to stay at Holkham, also came up to Scotland where we were living in lodges on the estate. She was trained up as a VAD nurse because the main house, Cortachy Castle, had been requisitioned as part of the war effort as a rehabilitation centre for Polish soldiers. The soldiers all seemed so glamorous in their uniforms and high boots and on their days off, the VADs changed into pretty cotton dresses and they used to go on picnics together, like the one described by Aunt Sylvia in her piece.

Picnic with the Poles, 1941
Sylvia Combe

In the hot summer of 1941 many Polish soldiers found themselves in Angus, Scotland, after the fall of France. Members of the Tenth Mounted Rifle Regiment, they were very brave and gallant, good company and excellent dancers. They had a great success with the local females, though perhaps were not so popular with the males! There was Bridget's Pole, Sophie's Pole, Peggy's Pole, etc., etc. Communication was carried on in indifferent but voluble French, and a good time was had by all.

Some of the officers used to come for evening picnics held on the edge of Lintrathan Loch, a lovely lake surrounded by pine woods with distant views of the Grampian Hills. Food was scarce in those days of rationing, and quite often the picnic was delayed until the hens had laid enough eggs. Luckily the Poles were well laden with booze, which they drank in incredible mixtures – whisky, gin and sherry all together – but they had very strong heads and were never the worse for wear. After one merry evening by the loch one of the most attractive of the officers, called Richard, plunged in for a refreshing swim. He had not realised that he was swimming in the Dundee water supply reservoir, and was chased by two irate Water Board officials in a boat – and that, sadly, was the last of the Polish picnics by the lake.

Baked Omelette

> eggs, beaten
> seasoning
> chopped herbs
> finely chopped onion
> finely chopped bacon or chicken

Preheat the oven to gas mark 7 (425°F, 220°C). Mix all the ingredients together. Bake in buttered shallow containers (I use small enamel plates) as many very thin, individual omelettes as required. Fold in half when cold. Freshly potted shrimps or asparagus tips may be added before folding.

Elizabeth Leicester

My sisters Carey, Sarah and I all adored our mother. When we were young she used to plan the most wonderfully exciting things to do in the holidays and would do them all with us, whether it was camping or climbing trees; my school friends all thought she was marvellous. I think perhaps because she was only nineteen years older than me she was a bit like a lovely big sister. When I was seven she went with my father to Egypt where he had been posted with the Scots Guards in the war. I remember her telling me I had to look after Carey when she was gone, which I did in a rather bossy way, poor Carey. But they were away for three years, which is really quite a long time at that age and I remember when they came back we hid behind our beloved governess Billy Williams' skirts because we were shy and only really remembered our parents from photographs. It didn't take long for our mother to win back our affections. I think she had had a pretty wild time in Egypt, she was only twenty-five or -six and very pretty and there were lots of glamorous parties and gymkhanas and picnics in the desert. She wouldn't have had any choice about going. In those days wives just went with their husbands, the children took a back seat. She was resourceful though. She started the pottery at Holkham, inspired by a prisoner of war from the camp set up on the estate who had built his own pottery wheel and kiln. I showed absolutely no aptitude for the artistic side of making the mugs and butter dishes, but I was really keen to sell and was aware of the need to try and make money for the estate. She allowed me to go on sales trips around the coast to all the fancy gift shops, selling Holkham pottery, sometimes staying with friends but often just in the hotels frequented by travelling salesmen. It seems quite a brave thing to do now, but I never had any trouble and in fact the other salesmen were often friendly and helpful to me. She was also very funny and I love the picnic she wrote about: the shooting party dinner which ends with the poor man sitting next to her going home 'as hungry at the end of the meal as he had been at the beginning!'

Holkham Shooting Lunches
Elizabeth Leicester

Holkham shooting lunches in the 1920s were spartan, to say the least. The Lord Leicester of the day was so keen on the sport that eating was considered a great waste of time. I remember in the early 1930s, one Christmas in deep snow, going out to find the trestle table in a wood. On it were a loaf of bread, a rather hollow Stilton and the famous box of small, raw Spanish onions – a Holkham tradition even today. Their strength cannot be exaggerated; there was not a dry eye round the table and a great deal of nose-blowing went on. The eagerly awaited moment produced a small glass of port, which brought some life back into frozen hands and feet.

In later years there were great improvements – lunch indoors with soup, Irish stew and treacle tart kept hot round a blazing fire, with a welcoming drink for each guest.

But the most unusual Holkham dish is velvet. There is a herd of deer in Holkham Park. In the autumn the stags shed a thick skin from their antlers which is collected, fried and served on toast. This delicacy is known as velvet, and was much prized by Lord Leicester who ate it as a savoury. Once at a dinner party we ladies proceeded to the great North Dining-room in full evening dress and wearing long kid gloves, each on the arm of a gentleman in white tie and tails. My partner was very old, nearly blind and deaf. The first course was cockles. Being undercooked, their shells hadn't opened, so had to be speared with a fork until one gave up with badly bleeding fingers. Suckling pig, then on to the velvet, while a loud and spirited explanation of its origin went on as it congealed on the plate. My neighbour was as hungry at the end of the meal as he had been at the beginning!

Vegetable Pie

(for four approximately)

This superb dish I have never seen in any recipe book or eaten outside our family circle, so, if you get it right, you are in for a treat! We have never used weights and measures for this pie, so I hope the directions below will prove a success the first time.

- 6 medium-sized potatoes, cooked
- 2–3 medium onions, sliced and lightly fried
- 2–3 hard-boiled eggs, sliced

    3 tomatoes, sliced
    4 cupfuls cooked spaghetti broken into 3-inch lengths
    1 pint béchamel sauce
    salt
    pepper
    butter

In a deep pie dish arrange a layer of sliced potatoes, sprinkle on some of the fried onion, slices of egg, tomatoes, and spaghetti. Pour a generous quantity of béchamel over and season with salt and pepper. Continue this layering, ending with potatoes. Dot with butter and put in medium oven for 15–20 minutes. Finish off under the grill until potatoes are brown.

It is important to have plenty of sauce. This can have different flavourings. One that is excellent is 1 cup of tomato sauce, ½ teaspoon mixed spice and half a dried chilli stirred into the béchamel.

Anne Glenconner

It was quite difficult for me to write about a picnic as family, Colin and friends had written about Holkham, Glen and Mustique, so I thought I would draw on the memories of a former kitchen maid for the preparation of a picnic shooting lunch. Holkham is now open to the public and I often hear the visitors' comments when they come into the Old Kitchen and see the gleaming brass containers for the picnic. They always wonder what they are for!

Preparations for a Shooting Picnic at Holkham
Anne Glenconner

On Thursday, 21 June 1979, Mrs Taylor, who had been a kitchen maid at Holkham from 1918 to 1920, returned to the house on a visit. Born Gladys Barlow in 1900, during her time as a housemaid she was never allowed in the state rooms, although on one occasion, when the family was away, a housemaid smuggled her along the ground-floor passages to peep into the Marble Hall for a few seconds. This was considered a very daring act which would have been punished if seen by any of the senior staff. Seven full-time footmen worked in the house and, when in their best livery, the powdered footmen wore black suits, yellow and black check waistcoats and white gloves. On occasions additional footmen were sent over on loan from Lord Lothian of Blickling Hall. Other staff included four kitchen maids, two kitchen porters, nine housemaids, two still-room maids and five laundry maids.

A whole carcass of lamb, calf or deer would be cooked for the household, the best cuts for the dining room or shooting picnic, next for the nursery, then senior and junior staff. One man would spend his day preparing vegetables, including a hundred weight (50 kg) of potatoes a day.

In the old kitchen Mrs Taylor pointed out three steamers in the recess to the right of the spit and said they were not used every day for cooking, but only for shooting lunches. The steam would be generated in the boiler below (now an incinerator) and the steamer would be used to cook fish and meat, with the four small containers for vegetables.

Shortly before midday the game cart would arrive at the porter's door and footmen would disconnect the unions of the steamers, which were then carried to the game cart and transported to wherever lunch was being taken. Church Paddock and Scarborough Clump were favourite places.

The rules of the kitchen were such that no unauthorised person was allowed in, and for this reason the serving hatches on either side of the kitchen door were regularly in use – one for hot food and the other for cold. The main door was not used.

Another interesting memory features the boiled egg for the children's breakfast. At about eight o'clock each morning two footmen would arrive in the kitchen with a trolley. On the trolley was a large copper container into which boiling water would be poured. An inner liner was then placed inside and this in turn would receive a number of fresh eggs. More boiling water was poured in until the eggs were completely covered. The whole was then covered with a lid and the trolley pushed from the kitchen to the nursery in the Chapel wing. The timing was such that on arrival the eggs were freshly boiled and ready for the children's breakfast.

I had great difficulty in choosing two recipes from my grandmother's own recipe book. There were so many good ones. Finally I decided on Holkham Pudding, which I have never had anywhere else, and a delicious venison dish which travels well and has been much appreciated when I have produced it on picnics in Scotland.

Holkham Pudding

> 6 oz (175 g) sifted self-raising flour
> 8 oz (225 g) shredded suet
> 2 eggs
> 6 oz (175 g) sultanas
> 5 oz (150 g) soft brown sugar
> 1 small cup of milk
> a little caster sugar

Mix all the ingredients, except the caster sugar, and beat on the lowest setting of the electric whisk for 2 minutes. Leave for 1 hour. Place in a buttered pudding basin and steam for 2 hours, then turn out on an ovenproof serving dish and sprinkle with caster sugar. Bake in a hot oven for thirty minutes. Serve with hot melted butter and chilled. This pudding tastes good cut into slices and fried in hot butter or eaten cold like a cake.

Venison Chops with Chestnut Purée

> 6 venison chops
> 1 teaspoon salt
> ½ teaspoon pepper
> 1 tablespoon butter

Purée
> 1 lb (450 g) chestnuts
> ½ pint (275 ml) stock
> milk to blend until right consistency is reached
> 1 oz (25 g) butter

Sauce
> 3 tablespoons redcurrant jelly
> juice of 4 oranges

Neatly trim and flatten the chops, season all over with salt and pepper. Thoroughly heat butter in a pan and add the chops. Cook for 6 minutes on each side.

Split the chestnut skins at the pointed ends and put the chestnuts into a saucepan. Cover them with water and bring to the boil. Take them out of the water and skin them. Put them back in the pan with just enough stock to cover and simmer for an hour. Purée them by mashing with hot milk and butter. Place the purée in the middle of a dish and arrange the chops round them.

Remove fat from the first pan, add redcurrant jelly and mix

thoroughly until melted. Pour in orange juice, mix well, and boil for 2 minutes. Pour the sauce over the chops.

When the dish is taken on a picnic, the chestnut purée and sauce should be carried in separate containers.

Carey Basset

Carey like my mother was very artistic, she did art at City & Guilds and helped my mother to design the wonderful patterns for Holkham pottery. She had three sons, sadly one of whom died, but the youngest son, James, lives near me in Norfolk and he and my son Christopher, who are close in age, went to the same prep school and are great friends. Carey adored coming out to Mustique and Colin used to find fantastic costumes for her to wear to his fancy dress parties. We had a very happy holiday together travelling around the islands of the Caribbean. You can tell from her picnic what fun she was. I love the thought of her pretending thunderflies in the mayonnaise was actually an accident with black pepper – that was typical of her sense of humour.

Carey's Cold Collation
Carey Basset

No doubt you will think that this is an appallingly badly planned menu, and you would be right; however, try it for easiness's sake and a saving on the electricity bill. And try to arrange the picnic near somebody else's fruit orchard or garden, so that guests who are sober enough to walk can pick their own pudding.

The day of my trial picnic coincided with a plague of a million tiny thunderflies; however, I pretended I had had an accident with the black pepper while making the mayonnaise, so nobody was any the wiser.

The menu is enough for four people. With the quantities given in the recipe you will get 28 small profiteroles, 4 savoury and 3 sweet for each person. The profiteroles go soft the day after they are made, so crisp them up in a very hot oven for 4 or 5 minutes. They are best eaten fresh. Taking paper plates and cups saves washing up; knives and forks aren't needed, but paper napkins are essential as one's fingers smell awful after peeling prawns.

PS. Don't forget to take water for the dogs.

Picnic Puffs

> 7½ fl. oz (220 ml) water
> 3 oz (75 g) butter
> 3½ oz (85 g) plain flour
> 3 eggs
> baking sheets

Preheat the oven to gas mark 7 (425°F, 220°C). Put the water and butter into a fairly large saucepan. Sift the flour. Bring the pan to the boil and when bubbling draw aside. Allow the bubbles to subside, then pour in all the flour at once. Stir vigorously with a wooden spoon until the mixture comes cleanly away from the sides of the pan – this happens very quickly. Allow to cool for 5 minutes and then transfer the mixture to a Magimix bowl with the double-bladed steel knife already in position. Switch on the machine and add the eggs one by one, processing after each addition until the mixture is smooth. If you don't own a Magimix you will have to beat by hand, but I must admit I've never tried it the hard way. Grease the baking sheet or sheets and hold under the cold tap; shake off surplus water. Place teaspoons of the mixture on the sheets, leaving room for expansion, and bake for about 20 minutes. If you have an Aga, as I do, place the sheets first in the baking oven, and finish in the roasting oven for the same times as given above. When baked, put on a wire rack to cool and pierce the sides with a skewer to let the steam escape, otherwise the profiteroles will be soggy inside.

Some Savoury Fillings

> Scrambled egg with smoked salmon or anchovy pieces
> Prawns or shrimps in mayonnaise
> Lobster or crab in mayonnaise
> Minced beef or other minced meats, and onion
> Diced raw vegetables in mayonnaise
> Cream cheese on lettuce leaves
> Ham, mustard and parsley
> Diced bacon and tomatoes
> Caviar and sour cream

It's best to let people assemble their own fillings and not risk soggy profiteroles. However, the chocolate ones travel well.

Chocolate Puffs

> 4 oz (110 g) bar plain chocolate
> whipped cream

Melt the chocolate with a little water or liquid coffee in a double boiler or a basin placed over hot (not boiling) water. Split the profiteroles and fill with whipped cream. Spoon the chocolate over the tops.

Christopher Tennant

As anyone who has read *Lady in Waiting* will know my son Christopher had a terrible accident when he was nineteen, as a result of which he is disabled. He hasn't been able to work, although he's done quite a bit for the charity Headway. His lovely wife Johanna mentioned that he would like to write about what it's like for a disabled person to try and picnic, which I thought was a really good idea. He also wanted to write about Boopa who was the elephant Colin had on St Lucia, so I'm delighted we can include his picnic in this edition of the book.

A Picnic with Boopa
Christopher Tennant

Picnics have always been a big part of my life and from an early age I have memories of simple picnics by the dark, still waters of the Loch at Glen Estate as well as more opulent picnics on the white sand beaches of Mustique.

They were always fun but none more so that in 1980 when

we went with my father Colin to visit his newly purchased land in St Lucia, the Jalousie Estate. Acres of undeveloped forests and open grassy glades leading down to the crystal clear, turquoise sea.

Mum, Amy, May and I piled into Dad's old Range Rover, which had certainly seen better days, and he drove us up along a rough track by the edge of the sea, over a concrete bridge, then turned the vehicle down a steep hill and headed up an old, almost impassable, rutted, riverbed. The gears crunched, the engine revved but eventually we reached the top where there was the most incredible view looking out over the whole estate. Not a comfortable ride but well worth it!

We drove on a bit further until we reached a flat plateau of green grass where the old, now derelict, Estate House sat proudly – surrounded by old stone walls – facing out to the sea.

Mum, May, Amy and I disembarked and ran down towards the sea for a swim when suddenly, we heard a rustling in the bushes and to our amazement and excitement, a tiny baby elephant poked its head out. 'Meet Boopa,' Colin said. We were lost for words!

We swam whilst Boopa looked on from the shore, then walked back to the old house where our picnic of bread rolls, cheese, salad and fried flying fish had been laid out on the grass by Mr T. Boy and his wife, Mona. Boopa came close to the wall and stuck her trunk over, sniffing around looking for food, much to our amusement and delight. When the Banana Cream was served for pudding, she must have caught a whiff of the bananas as she stretched her trunk out as far as it could possibly reach, in an effort to sample its delights.

It was a truly magical day and one that I will never forget. Dad was a master of surprises!

★

When I met my wife Johanna, she asked me how I had coped following my accident to which I replied, 'There are not many advantages to being disabled, but the few advantages there are, I take full advantage of.'

Picnics these days are not so glamorous but, nevertheless, still great fun and a situation where I can take full advantage! Since my accident it can be challenging, to say the least, to traverse fields or any uneven ground to get to the site of a picnic. Sitting on the grass is impossible because it takes ages to get up again and requires a lot of pulling and pushing from the other guests, so the alternative is to sit in those dreadful canvas folding picnic chairs, which are far too small to fit my frame into and they always sink into the ground or fold up around me! So someone always drives me as close as they can get to where the picnic is being held. I can drink my rum straight from the bottle on the basis it is easier than trying to manage a glass, no one bats an eyelid when I eat with my hands instead of using a knife and fork, and when in need of a quick 'leak' I can just head off towards the nearest bush without anyone raising an eyebrow – though I rarely make it there on time!

Fried Flying Fish

    8 flying fish fillets
    1½ teaspoon salt
    juice of 1 large lime
    1 clove of garlic crushed
    1 teaspoon chopped chives
    1 small onion – grated
    ½ teaspoon marjoram
    1 dash of hot pepper sauce

60 g flour
¼ teaspoon cayenne pepper
salt and a large pinch of black pepper
1 egg, lightly beaten
60 g of breadcrumbs or cornflakes crumbed
butter for frying
2 limes for garnish

Place the fish fillets in a shallow bowl and season with salt and lime juice and set aside for 30 mins.

Drain and pat the fish dry on paper towel. In a small mixing bowl mix garlic, chives, onion, marjoram and hot pepper sauce together and rub the mixture on the fillets.

Mix the flour, cayenne pepper, salt and pepper in a shallow dish. Dip the fillets in the egg and then the flour and bread- or cornflake crumbs.

Heat the butter in a frying pan and cook the fillets for 3 minutes on each side until lightly browned.

Garnish with lime wedges and serve.

Kelvin O'Mard

Kelvin was a close friend of my son Henry. He is an actor who has worked for the Royal Shakespeare Company, the Bristol Old Vic and the Royal Court Theatre, among others. He was in a film called *Water* starring Michael Caine, which was shot in St Lucia in 1984, and not long after that he met Henry. They became really good friends, bonding in the first instance over their love of St Lucia. They were both Buddhists and when Henry was dying of AIDS, Kelvin was right there with him, looking after him together with Henry's then estranged wife Tessa. Henry adored them both. Kelvin became a firm friend of the family; he always comes to our celebrations and is a very special person. I asked him to contribute a picnic in which he could write about his first impressions of Henry and all of us and I think he's written something rather moving.

Anne Glenconner

A Caribbean Picnic on Bequia
Kelvin O'Mard

Friendship has always been a very important aspect of my life, ever since I was a small boy growing up in the East End of London during the 1960s. Whether it was climbing trees to pick apples in a neighbour's garden, playing hopscotch or galavanting on the local Hackney marshes, I was always with that special person, a 'best friend' with whom I felt I shared an important bond. This was most certainly the case when I met the tall and dashing Henry Tennant with whom I shared the most special of friendships. I met Henry during the 1980s, through our mutual love of the Caribbean and a coincidental meeting that to this day I believe was written in the stars.

I had just returned from the island of St Lucia where I had just finished making the 1984 film *Water* that starred the legendary actor Sir Michael Caine. I played the rather accident prone Nado, houseboy to Sir Michael Caine's 'Governor Thwaite'. It is a role I cherish to this day and during my first ever conversation with Henry, I discovered that most of the film was shot on land on the Island of St Lucia just below the Pitons, an area that was owned by Henry's father Lord Glenconner. Henry and I would talk for hours about the Caribbean and although coming from different ends of the social spectrum, we found common ground that rested on a love of the Caribbean islands that sit close to the equator, and are surrounded by turquoise seas and bathed in glorious sunlight. It was not a surprise to learn that Henry's father, Colin Tennant, had bought the island of Mustique in the Grenadines, where history now tells the story of lavish parties and where the rich and famous established holiday homes. Most notably Princess Margaret who was gifted a stretch of land on

Mustique as a wedding present. Henry loved Mustique for its golden beaches and its remoteness and it was a place where he seemed to find himself and where he was most relaxed.

I first visited Mustique in 1986 for Colin's sixtieth birthday party. It was the party of all parties, where the celebrations lasted for four or five days. The Windstar, a sixty-berth yacht with computerised sails, ferried Colin's guests around in the most luxurious comfort. The celebrations included a treasure hunt on the island of Bequia, the largest of the islands that make up the Grenadines archipelago. The treasure hunt took Colin's guests on a wonderful mystery tour of the island, where we had to solve a clue before we could move on to the next point of the adventure. It was during this treasure hunt that Henry and I came across, and fell in love with, the village Paget Farm, which seemed stuck in time and one could describe as almost biblical. The people who live there were very friendly. After Colin's party, Henry and I decided to stay on in the Caribbean and we rented a house in Paget Farm, overlooking the sea and from which we could see Mustique in the distance. We made friends with the local fishermen who were only too happy to take us on excursions in their coloured fishing boats to neighbouring islands, all of which were uninhabited. They took us to Bird Island, which derives its name from the multitude of beautiful birds that have made the island their home, among them the tropical mockingbird, hummingbirds with their blue and green iridescent plumage and the forked-tailed, prehistoric looking frigatebirds. Surrounded by sandy beaches on one side of the island and fierce looking rocks on the other, this was to be the setting for our Caribbean picnic.

Henry and I were ferried to Bird Island in a brightly coloured motor boat, skippered by two local fishermen, Nick and Danis, who had taken it upon themselves to be our tour guides and who also provided the picnic that was concealed in a cold box and would be cooked once we had landed. On the menu was a light fish stew made with fish caught that day and spicy jerk chicken that we roasted over a barbecue.

Once we had landed on the beach, our fishermen friends immediately set about building the barbecue and lighting it, placing a small pot with water at one end. Leaving Henry and myself on the beach to tend to the fire, Nick and Danis went back to the boat, which they took a few metres out to sea and from which they dived into the water. When each appeared they gleefully held up a handful of small fish which were quickly cleaned and added to the now boiling water. A little salt was added, black pepper and pimento seeds. They also added a few small diced potatoes, a carrot and some roughly fashioned dumplings, affectionately known in the Caribbean as 'droppers'. I was keen to see what else our fishermen friends were going to pull out of their cold box. And was pleased to see they had also brought along a few beers.

The jerk chicken had been prepared the night before and was sitting in a plastic Tupperware. The pieces of chicken were placed on the barbecue, hissing and sending a waft of spicy loveliness into the air. Each piece of chicken would be carefully turned so they would be evenly cooked and not burned, and basted with a barbecue sauce which had also magically appeared from the generous cold box.

The fish stew was delicious. It was fresh and light almost like a French bouillabaisse, however with dumplings. It was the perfect starter while we waited for the jerk chicken to be properly cooked. When it was ready, the chicken was served with a simple side salad of lettuce, cucumber and coleslaw and Caribbean hard dough bread. The pieces of chicken we ate with our fingers, ensuring to pluck every morsel of the spicy flesh from the bone.

It was, as we were told by Nick and Danis, the only way to eat jerk chicken. Everything was washed down by the beers we had brought and had kept cool in the shallows.

Henry and I were to have many picnics while living on Bequia, a place where our friendship was to be sealed by such beautiful memories.

Mary Ann Sieghart

One of my closest friends is called Tim Leese. He's a garden designer and now lives with his partner in the old head gardener's house at Holkham, so I see him often. When I was writing *Lady in Waiting* he'd come and cook for me – every evening there was a delicious supper waiting, he was so kind. When his mother was on her deathbed, she told Tim that the person he had always thought was his father was not his father but in fact was Paul Sieghart. So suddenly Tim had a whole new family and Mary Ann is his half-sister, which is how I know her. We had a lovely time together at the Chalk Valley Literary Festival, which has one of the nicest green rooms of anywhere I've been, a wonderful tent all done up with comfy sofas and flowers and buffet food. She's such a brilliant journalist and talented writer that I was very keen she write a piece and I love her Poachers Picnic.

The Poacher's Pocket Picnic
Mary Ann Sieghart

I love going to the theatre, but detest the timing of it. With curtain up at 7.30 p.m., how on earth are we supposed to eat? As we normally have supper at about 8 p.m. or 8.30 p.m., I can't summon an appetite for a pre-theatre dinner at the infants' eating hour of 6 p.m. And with plays getting longer and longer, nor can I wait until we return home at about 10.30 p.m. I'd either faint with hunger during the show or annoy my neighbours with the rumbling of my stomach.

So what's the solution? The Poacher's Pocket Picnic. You assemble a small picnic that – together with an appropriate bottle – fits into the inside poacher's pocket of your husband's coat. He can then walk nonchalantly into the theatre, past the security guards checking bags, with the interval food and drink nicely stashed and undetected.

The Poacher's Pocket Picnic also solves the other theatre problem: the prohibitive cost of food and drink. Who wants to pay upwards of £15 a glass for nasty champagne or £10 a glass for even nastier wine, when you can bring a much nicer entire bottle of your own? Moreover, it saves on queues at the bar. While your fellow audience members are spending half the interval waiting to be served and the other half waiting to pee, you can be happily tucking into your PPP.

The only question is, where to eat it. At the National Theatre, there's no problem. Nobody seems to mind punters bringing in their own Tupperware. If the weather's nice, you can eat and drink on one of the balconies overlooking the Thames.

At less democratic theatres, however, you have to be rather more discreet to evade the food-and-drink police. We usually try to grab a table in the furthest corner of the bar area, pour our own drinks and hide the bottle away. We then hope they won't object to our eating our own sandwiches.

Once, though, we tried something rather more ambitious. We had seats in the gods with a rather poor view of the stage. We had a very good view, though, of an empty box, which seemed to be going to waste. So, in the interval, we found our way to the box and tried the door, which was miraculously unlocked. What a great place to eat our sandwiches and drink our champagne undisturbed!

Once ensconced, we wondered whether we dared watch the second half from these much better seats. No one was a loser, we calculated: the box would otherwise be empty, and it made no difference to the theatre whether we sat there or not. Indeed, the actors would feel less demoralised with fewer empty seats in their view. So we decided to hold our nerve and stay.

We counted down the minutes to the end of the interval, praying that we would remain unnoticed. And then, just before the lights came down, there was a knock at the door. Aghast, my husband quickly hid the champagne bottle as a uniformed member of staff came in. We had been bubbled! We were certain to be reprimanded and marched out of the theatre in disgrace. I held my breath and smiled sweetly at the theatre attendant, who merely smiled sweetly back and asked me to take my glass off the red velvet shelf in front of me, in case it fell on to an audience member below. And that was that! We enjoyed the second half all the more for the illicit satisfaction of having got away with it.

And what are the ingredients of a PPP? A bottle of chilled white Burgundy or fizz, a couple of smoked salmon and cream cheese sandwiches and a bar of seventy per cent dark chocolate. Easy to stash, easy to eat and easy to hide away. Curtains up!

Rupert Everett

I have known Rupert since he was born as I was a great friend of his mother and was one of her bridesmaids when she got married. I have huge admiration for Rupert as an actor and writer. His performance in *The Judas Kiss* as Oscar Wilde I thought was wonderful and his memoirs were both so amusing and brilliantly written. He is also one of the kindest and funniest people I know.

Bird Island Picnic
Rupert Everett

As a child, my second home was my grandparents' house at Burnham Deepdale on the north coast of Norfolk.

I had been born there and the cornerstone of my character – such as it is – was formed in the freezing north-easterly wind that blew in over the marsh. It was my favourite place in the world.

As soon as spring came my grandparents ate their meals outside and in the summer months, depending on the tide and the barometer, we might set off for a picnic to Bird Island, reachable at low tide on foot, leaving the house in a long line, through the gate at the bottom of the poplar wood and up on to the bank that held the marsh and the sea at bay from the fields and woods of Holkham. The view had not changed since Nelson looked at it. The men peeled off towards my grandfather's boat, moored in the creek, laden down with big blue bags filled with sails, rollocks and batons, while the women walked in single file along the bank, my mother, my aunts, my grandmother, my great-grandmother and their best friend, a lady called Audrey Earle, in a huge Mexican hat. They carried the picnic. I danced ahead with my shrimping net or lagged behind picking samphire from the evil smelling marsh.

Once on Bird Island the tide quickly turned and it was cut off from the mainland, which was thrilling for us children. We sat on tartan rugs in the dunes (out of the wind) and ate cold sausages, samphire and hard-boiled eggs. The grown-ups drank wine while we sipped hot Bovril from a thermos. After the meal we had to wait for an hour before going into the ice-cold sea, swimming and shrimping, in snorkels and armbands, followed by more Bovril, as we sat shivering in stripey towels. Then the whole picnic was carefully packed up again and we got into Grandpa's boat and sailed home, tacking through the creeks while he shouted 'Ready about... Leo' and we all ducked as the boom swung.

Graham Norton

One of the lovely things about *Lady in Waiting* was being asked to go on all these television shows, but it really started with Graham. Graham's been wonderful. I met him first when I was on his Radio 2 programme. I've noticed how quite often the presenter hasn't read the book, but Graham obviously had read *Lady in Waiting*, and we got on very well. At the end of the interview I rather boldly mentioned that I'd love to be on his red sofa. Fortunately, Season Three of *The Crown* had just come out and both Helena Bonham Carter and Nancy Carroll, who played me, had come to see me to talk about it. Helena told me she was going to be on *The Graham Norton Show* and very luckily they felt they wanted me on as well. I had to wait until half time to appear and I was frightfully nervous waiting backstage, looking at them all on the television in the Green Room. I was quite anxious about climbing up the ladder to get on to the stage but Graham came to help me, which was nice. Rupert Everett had said to me, 'Graham loves a bit of sexual innuendo. You should just go straight in with your honeymoon story.' So that's what I did pretty much as soon as I sat down, I just launched into it. I think Graham was slightly surprised, but the audience seemed to love it. It was all great fun, and afterwards Chadwick Boseman, who has now sadly died, came up to me and just said, 'Gee whizz, Lady,' which I though was hilarious! The programme helped me to reach a wider audience which was so nice. I've kept in touch with Graham and he has very kindly contributed a 'non' picnic which I love.

A Patch of Blue Sky
Graham Norton

Growing up in Ireland during the sixties and seventies I reacted to British picnics with a mixture of awe and bewilderment. My parents had a caravan on the coast of West Cork and that was where we would spend our summers. Walking along the road to the beach we would occasionally see a car with a UK sticker parked by a grassy patch above the cliffs and we would stare at the tourists eating their meal. Small tables were erected and to the side wicker hampers, like Mary Poppins' handbag, would disgorge plates, cutlery and glassware. The British picnickers, dexterous as magicians, would produce piles of Tupperware boxes more intricate than any Russian dolls. Whole meals would be carefully assembled and washed down with actual wine! These were picnics for Instagram before that particular portal to hell existed. Picture perfect but, in reality, far from ideal. Napkins and loose leaves of lettuce would be carried over the cliffs by the stiff sea breeze, uncomfortable fold-out chairs wobbled precariously on the uneven ground, and the whole meal was consumed while being laid siege by an assortment of seagulls, wasps and pigeons. We shook our heads. If that was how you wanted to eat, surely you should be doing it indoors?

As far as I recall, every summer, we ate all our meals sitting at the flimsy Formica-covered table inside our caravan. We may have opened the windows but that was as al fresco as we got. The most that was consumed outdoors might have been an ice cream or an unripe blackberry found in a hedgerow. What we thought of as picnics were reserved for long drives and had more to do with economy than culinary pleasure. These *picnics* tended to be enjoyed in the car with the doors open. Salad sandwiches with salad cream seeping through the bread would be followed by something sweet, perhaps a slice of fruit loaf and then, if God was good, a packet of Tayto potato crisps. This was usually washed down by some pre-diluted *MiWadi* served in a bottle that bore the label of something we would have much preferred, such as orange lemonade.

If we did venture outside to eat it was always spontaneous. Coats thrown on the ground, a hastily purchased sausage roll, actual fizzy drinks reassuringly made in a factory. Now this might sound dismal, but the beauty of such picnics was that our expectations were low. If it started to rain, or we noticed platoons of ants marching up the sleeve of our makeshift picnic blanket, nothing was lost. We might not have had as nice a time as we had hoped but we could just walk away with no regrets. The tourists by the cliff were struggling to find the right lid for the Tupperware. The table leg wouldn't fold down, their elaborate cream cake was now just sludge on a plate. It seems to me, even now after living in the UK for nearly forty years, that planning a picnic is deciding to be disappointed.

For me, the only recipe anyone needs for a successful picnic is to see a patch of blue in the sky that is, as my father used to say, 'big enough for a pair of sailor's trousers' and then pop into the nearest garage shop and stock up on some items packed with fat and salt. Consume these snacks somewhere you can at least see a tree and count yourself one of the luckiest people alive.

Lorraine Kelly

I was sitting in my dressing room at the TV Studios in London before going on Lorraine's programme to promote *Lady in Waiting*. I was having my hair and make-up done. I love all that, the false eyelashes and everything. Lorraine came in and I liked her straight away. She said she was really looking forward to talking to me and told me roughly what she was going to ask, and it was all a very nice experience. Since then I've been on her show four times. I've only met Lorraine in the studio but she's always been so incredibly nice, and was very kind to write a picnic piece for the book, which is a lovely evocation of her childhood.

A Seaside Picnic
Lorraine Kelly

When I think back to my childhood summer days, they are always illuminated in a sort of golden sunny haze of playing outdoors, and going to the seaside for picnics.

We lived in a tenement in the East End of Glasgow and it was a massive treat to take a weekend day trip to the seaside at Ayr, Troon or Seamill.

My mum would make big fat generous sandwiches out of a 'Vienna loaf', which she'd hollow out and stuff full of chicken, lettuce and mayonnaise (hugely posh and sophisticated back in the sixties) and there would be home-made chocolate cornflake cakes and potato scones lathered in butter.

When we had put up the stripy windbreaker near 'our' rock at the beach, we'd spread the tartan blanket, run into the sea for a paddle and then gorge on the goodies from my mum's old picnic basket.

Everything tasted so much better when eating out in the open, even in a gale with the threat of horizontal rain. The paper plates flew away and the hard-boiled eggs were gritty with sand, but we didn't care.

I had to keep an eye on my little brother Graham who, although he was six years younger than me, ate like a tiny piglet and always managed to snaffle all the 'Blue Riband' biscuits.

There were always other families to play with, either building sandcastles, searching for crabs in the rock pools or playing endless games of football where we made up the rules as we went along.

Our picnic feast was made even more special with pokey hats (ice-cream cones with a chocolate flake and red sweet sauce) and sticks of rock that ruined our teeth.

I'm sure it must have rained and we would have been freezing after being in the cold salty sea, and I bet my brother and I fought like scratchy cats in a basket. My poor mum must have been exhausted getting up early to prepare the food, keeping us amused and then clearing up afterwards, as well as trying to stop us beating each other up, but I remember those picnics with huge affection.

My mum gave us brilliant memories, and a love of eating al fresco that I enjoy to this day when we are off camping in the wilds of Zimbabwe or Botswana, and the sandwiches and cakes still taste better outdoors.

Gyles Brandreth

Gyles is a great admirer of royalty and friend of the Queen's. I first met him when he interviewed me onstage at Alexandra Palace. He turned up in this fabulous jumper which had crowns all over it. It was really quite a long talk with an interval in the middle, but he got the audience involved and we all laughed a lot. Afterwards I said how lovely that there were so many people there and how smart all the ladies looked in their hats, and he said, 'They aren't ladies.' It turned out they were all men in drag who came and chatted afterwards and wanted photographs taken with me. They said they imagined it's how I would have dressed as Lady-in-Waiting and I suppose they were right! One of the other joys of having written my book is that I've got quite a following among the gay community because of Henry and my work with HIV and AIDS charities. I've done several other events since then with Gyles, who very kindly agreed to write a picnic piece and sent a lovely photograph of his grandson with the Queen at the Mad Hatter's Tea Party.

Let Them Eat Cake
Gyles Brandreth

What have I brought to put in Lady Glenconner's picnic hamper? A cake. A royal cake, no less. Oh yes. When it comes to picnics, I like things to be done properly.

The first picnic, I suppose, was the one they had in the Garden of Eden. I can picture them, Adam and Eve, on a tartan rug, a few well-placed vine leaves protecting their modesty, enjoying an al fresco apple.

The first picnic I remember hearing about also featured in the Bible, but in the New Testament. I think the story of Jesus turning five loaves and two fishes into a feast for five thousand is not only the first miracle of his that is recorded, but is also the only one that features in each of the four Gospels. As a little boy in church, I do remember wondering how the miracle was achieved and being hugely impressed by the self-discipline of the five thousand because, famously, after the picnic there were several baskets of leftover food remaining. (In retrospect, I am glad not to have attended that particular picnic: crowds are not my thing. I have always avoided the Glastonbury Festival because of what can best be described as 'comfort break' anxieties.)

The first picnic that really set my imagination going was the one that took place on 4 July 1862. I wasn't there, but I have always wished that I had been. The Fourth of July 1862 was the day on which the Reverend Charles Lutwidge Dodgson, a mathematics don at Christ Church College, Oxford, better known to the world as the writer Lewis Carroll, with his friend, the Reverend Robinson Duckworth, set off on a rowing trip from Oxford to Godstow, with the three daughters of Henry Liddell, the Dean of Christ Church. The children were Lorina (known as Ina), Edith and Alice and it was on this expedition, at the picnic that the five of them enjoyed that afternoon on the riverbank, that Charles Dodgson extemporised the outline of the story that would become one of the most famous children's stories ever written.

Dodgson invented the tale for Alice Liddell and her sisters and, eventually, at Alice's insistence, wrote it down. In November 1864, when he was thirty-two and Alice was twelve, he presented her with a handwritten, illustrated manuscript entitled, *Alice's Adventures Underground*.

In 1863 he took the unfinished manuscript to a publisher who liked it immediately. After alternative titles were rejected – *Alice's Adventures Among the Fairies*, *Alice's Golden Hour* – the book was published in 1865, with illustrations by John Tenniel as *Alice's Adventures in Wonderland*. The rest is history, and I can claim a tiny part of it because, in the summer of 2023, I was honoured to unveil a small plaque on the Isis riverbank, marking the anniversary of the rowing trip and picnic that proved a landmark in the story of children's literature.

One of the most memorable scenes in the story, of course, is the Mad Hatter's Tea Party which, I reckon, is the best and certainly most fantastic outdoor picnic in all literature. A particular admirer of Alice, and the Mad Hatter, the March Hare and the Dormouse, was Queen Victoria who, according to legend, was so taken with Lewis Carroll's story that she commanded the author to dedicate his next book to her – and was accordingly presented with a scholarly mathematical volume entitled, *An Elementary Treatise on Determinants*.

Queen Victoria gave her name to the Victoria Sponge and, by several accounts, was partial to a slice of cake when out on a picnic herself. In Scotland, on picnics, she was also partial to the occasional cigarette – apparently to keep the midges at bay.

I know that Victoria's great-great-great-grandson Charles III also enjoys a picnic, as does his wife, Queen Camilla. I know this because Queen Camilla supports a number of projects to encourage reading, literacy, and the love of language – among them one that I instigated called Poetry Together, at which we bring older people and young people together for a poetry slam and a bit of a picnic. In fact, I have had the honour of attending a Poetry Together Mad Hatter's Tea Party with Her Majesty – at which my grandson, Rory, played the part of the Mad Hatter and the Queen brought her own cake.

> The old and the young went to tea
> With a beautiful home-made cake.
> It was Camilla's version of Victoria sponge,
> Delicious and easy to bake.
> The old and young learnt a poem by heart
> And performed it with their tea.
> 'Let's get together,' they said,
> 'Whatever the weather.'
> 'Let's get together,' they said,
> 'For poetry, cake and tea!'

That's what Poetry Together is all about – school-age children meeting up with elderly people at school or in care homes, performing a poem together that they have all learnt by heart – and having tea and cake. If you want to find out more about the project, take a look here: www.poetrytogether.com

If you fancy baking your own version of Queen Camilla's cake, Her Majesty has kindly supplied the recipe. Here it is:

Ingredients

    4 oz self-raising flour (110 g), sifted
    1 teaspoon baking powder
    4 oz (110 g) soft margarine or butter at room temperature
    4 oz (110 g) caster sugar
    2 large eggs
    2–3 drops of pure vanilla essence

To finish

    Lemon curd or jam (with fresh cream, optional) or
        Nutella or your filling of choice,
    and sifted icing sugar

Pre-heat the oven to gas mark 3 (325°F, 170°C).

Lightly grease two 7-inch (18 cm) sponge tins, no less than 1 inch (2.5 cm) deep and line with greaseproof paper (also greased) or silicone paper.

Take a large roomy mixing bowl and sift flour and baking powder into it, holding the sieve high to give the flour a good airing. Then simply add all the other ingredients to the bowl and whisk them – preferably with an electric hand whisk – till thoroughly combined. If the mixture doesn't drop off a wooden spoon easily when tapped on the side of the bowl, then add 1 or 2 teaspoons of tap-warm water, and whisk again.

Now divide the mixture between the two prepared tins, level off and bake on the centre shelf of the oven for about 30 minutes. When cooked leave them in the tins for only about 30 seconds, then loosen the edges by sliding a palette knife all round and turn them onto a wire cooling rack. Peel off the base papers carefully and, when cool, sandwich the cakes together with lemon curd or jam (or jam and fresh cream) or Nutella or your filling of choice, and dust with icing sugar.

(Queen Camilla loves poetry. And picnics. And chocolate, too. You can make a chocolate version of her cake if you prefer: simply omit the vanilla essence and add 1 tablespoon of cocoa powder to the basic ingredients.)

Cliff Parisi

My daughter-in-law Johanna used to work for Cliff many years ago when they both lived in north London and they have been friends ever since. Cliff played the character Minty Peterson in *Eastenders* for years and I was an avid fan, watching the show regularly. I decided to try and give up *Eastenders* but I do still watch *Call the Midwife* where he has played Fred Buckle, the caretaker, since 2012. When I celebrated my 80th birthday party at Holkham my children said they weren't going to let me drive myself, they were going to organise a driver to fetch me. I got ready and the car arrived – I suppose I wasn't really concentrating on the driver, probably worrying about not creasing my dress, although I did notice he was very smart and wearing a peaked cap. Eventually he said something to me and I looked up and he turned round and it was Cliff dressed up as a chauffeur! I couldn't quite believe it. He came in and joined the party and was absolutely mobbed by all my friends who are huge *Eastenders* fans. It was a fantastic surprise for everybody.

My Gi Tar Pic Nik
Cliff Parisi

I was bought up in north London and have absolutely no recollection of ever being taken on family picnics anywhere, not even to the local park. As a family, it was just not something we did.

I attended the local secondary school in the late seventies at a time when dyslexia was not recognised, so instead of receiving the help you needed, you were regarded as just being troublesome, disruptive and stupid. I was put in a class X where aside from suffering from dyslexia, many of the kids had extreme behavioural problems, so the classes were chaotic and I learned absolutely nothing! We were not allowed out of the classroom unless to go to the kitchen or the workshop as we were not trusted to move around the school on our own. Several years ago whilst clearing out some old boxes, I came across one of my old school reports. In all subjects there were comments from the teachers such as, 'If I knew what Cliff looked like, I might be able to write something'; 'Cliff is rarely present and does nothing when he is'; 'I am unable to report on Cliff's progress as he is rarely in class'!

So, it is no wonder, that by the age of twelve, instead of going into school, I would head to the bus stop outside the locals' favourite pub on Hornsey Rise, hop on the No.14 bus and travel down to Shaftesbury Avenue and London's Tin Pan Alley to the guitar shops.

I would spend all day looking at Fenders and Gibsons and from time to time a big car or van would pull up outside one of the shops and the musicians from a famous band like The Faces or T-Rex would pile out, head into the shop and buy a load of new equipment, often plugging in and jamming in the store. It was so much fun and better than being in school.

On the rare occasions I had any spare money, I would treat myself to a Bakewell Tart from a bakery or coffee shop and to this day, it is still my favourite cake and my idea of a perfect Pic Nik!

William Hanson

I thought it might be fun for someone to write about the 'correct' way to hold a picnic, if there is such a thing. William is an expert on and teacher of etiquette. I've always admired him when I've seen him on television and he's written several books. He sent me a proof of his latest book and on reading it I spotted one or two small mistakes so I told him and he was very grateful. I let him into a rule of thumb that Princess Margaret told me, which was never to use a French word when you can use an English one, it's such a brilliant piece of advice and immediately knocks out words like pardon and serviette. He thought that was rather good!

The Top Drawer Picnic
William Hanson

Long hot days, balmy evenings, dappled sunshine and lush meadows, soft plaid rugs, and leather-strapped wicker baskets: the perfect picnic may be the aspiration of summer outdoor entertaining, but the frisson of eating al fresco can quickly fizzle out if things don't run smoothly. Top-drawer picnic etiquette doesn't just happen; it culminates with copious consideration and plenty of practical planning.

First and foremost, comfort is king. While some rare souls are happy to eat lying down and digest horizontally, most of us left that with the Romans and prefer to sit on something upright. Picnic chairs are, therefore, a must, not only to avoid numb bums and aching limbs, but their built-in drink holders prevent unwanted spillages and nervy glass balancing. A chair also protects you from potentially hazardous surfaces, keeping food clean and eliminating the risk of sand or grass invading your plate. No one wants a sandy sausage or grassy bun.

A small picnic table should also be part of the inventory. There is no need to provide a full dining table but something just big enough to provide a solid surface for the serving dishes. A rug can also be laid down as a makeshift ground sheet, territory marker, and somewhere for those under eighteen to sit.

Call me a snob but plastic plates and cups are the sole reserve of children's birthday parties, and are never used by the enlightened in the way of decent picnic etiquette. (They are also horrid for the environment.) There are standards to be kept, so china plates and proper cutlery are essential hardware and much more eco-friendly. (Paper plates, also horrid, are, however, fine if you really can't be bothered with the washing-up.) Serving dishes should also be china and of smart buffet calibre; even if food is transported in Tupperware, there should be a quick, discreet and fuss-free transfer into something more stylish.

Food for a picnic par excellence is simple yet highly skilled. Present a spread of 1980s-inspired pork-heavy picnic fayre and your guests will be utterly underwhelmed and necking the antacids before bed. Instead, savvy hosts go for moreish, savoury munchettes that require little or no cutting – encouraging people to linger and graze – topped off with a pudding that is a touch indulgent or deliciously seasonal. After all, picnics are a time for slowing down and enjoying little luxuries and (seemingly) effortless deliciousness.

After getting this far, don't let the side down with inferior drinks and glassware. Hosts should bring a well-stocked selection (alcoholic and non-alcoholic) and a plentiful supply. It's surprising how thirsty everyone becomes when eating outdoors. If you are in pursuit of superior standards, then there would be ice to hand and bottles kept cool in wine coolers to save diving into the cool bag every time someone needs a top-up. Whether it's champagne, Chablis, cider or cola, no one wants it presented to them warm in a plastic glass. Leave the best crystal at home, but at the very least, serve drinks in decent glass glasses.

When the picnic is in full swing, hosts can sit back and admire their handy work (all the while keeping an eye on their guests' needs). After all, good etiquette and manners are all about consideration for others and bringing along a general sense of ease. Picnic planning is no different, really – perfect practicalities, fantastic food and delicious drinks, all in the hope that the weather behaves.

Rhubarb Shortbread

Shortbread ingredients
- 125 g butter, soft
- 125 g plain flour
- 25 g cornflour
- 2 level tablespoons of icing sugar

Topping ingredients

    250 g chopped rhubarb

    2 large eggs, beaten

    25 g plain flour

    200 g demerara sugar

    a few drops of vanilla essence

1 x 20 cm square tin, lined with foil and lightly greased

1. Preheat oven to 180°fan (200°C).
2. Mix butter, flours and icing sugar.
3. Press mixture into tin and prick with a fork.
4. Cook for 15–20 minutes.
5. Combine all the topping ingredients.
6. Pour onto base and return to oven for 40 minutes.
7. Allow to cool before removing from tin by foil. Cut into squares.

Picture Acknowledgements

Photographs produced courtesy of:

Pg 1: Top – Anne Glenconner
Bottom L and R - Anne Glenconner

Pg 2 - Top - Anne Glenconner
Middle - Violet Vyner
Bottom - Anne Glenconner

Pg 3 - Top - Anne Glenconner
Middle - Anne Glenconner
Bottom - Alban Donohoe

Pg 4 - Top - Christabel Holland
Middle - Anne Glenconner
Bottom - Mitch Crites

Pg 5 - Top - Rachel Johnson
Middle - Rachel Johnson
Bottom L and R - Anne Glenconner

Pg 6 - Top L - Charles Harding
Top R - Cliff Parisi
Middle - Milton Gendel, © Fondazione Primoli, Rome
Bottom R - Julian Sainsbury

Pg 7 - Top- By permission of the Earl of Leicester and the Trustees of the Holkham Estate
Middle - Anne Glenconner
Bottom - Anne Glenconner

Pg 8 - Top – Poetry Together
Bottom L - Anne Glenconner
Bottom R - Anne Glenconner

Every reasonable effort has been made to trace copyright holders, but if there are any errors or omissions, Bedford Square Publishers will be pleased to insert the appropriate acknowledgement in any subsequent printings or editions.

SafeLives

For too many people, home isn't a safe place and the people who are meant to love them, hurt them instead. Whether it's physical or psychological, abuse can happen to anyone, no matter where they live, how old they are, or what sort of lifestyle they have.

Thousands of survivors from all over the country have bravely shared their stories with SafeLives. Their experience tells us everything about the warning signs and the consequences of inaction. And their insight shows what works to keep victims and their families safe.

Together with survivors, SafeLives is transforming the response to domestic abuse and abusive relationships, so that those being harmed are made safer, sooner, and those doing the harming are held accountable.

If this has happened to you, or to a friend or family member, please know that you are not alone. There is help and support for you.

Domestic Abuse Helplines
- England 0808 2000 247
- Wales 080 80 10 800
- Scotland 0800 027 1234
- Northern Ireland 0808 802 1414

If you'd like to support SafeLives, please find more information at https://safelives.org.uk/support-us/

About the Author

Lady Glenconner was born Lady Anne Coke in 1932, the eldest daughter of the 5th Earl of Leicester, and grew up in their ancestral estate at Holkham Hall in Norfolk. A Maid of Honour at the Queen's Coronation, she married Lord Glenconner in 1956. They had 5 children together of whom 3 survive. In 1958 she and her husband began to transform the island of Mustique into a paradise for the rich and famous. They granted a plot of land to Princess Margaret who built her favourite home there. She was appointed Lady in Waiting to Princess Margaret in 1971 and kept this role — accompanying her on many state occasions and foreign tours — until her death in 2002. Lord Glenconner died in 2010, leaving everything in his will to his former employee. Her bestselling memoir *Lady in Waiting* was published in 2019, and she has written bestselling fiction. She now lives in a farmhouse near Kings Lynn in Norfolk.

Bedford Square Publishers is an independent publisher of fiction and non-fiction, founded in 2022 in the historic streets of Bedford Square London and the sea mist shrouded green of Bedford Square Brighton.

Our goal is to discover irresistible stories and voices that illuminate our world.

We are passionate about connecting our authors to readers across the globe and our independence allows us to do this in original and nimble ways.

The team at Bedford Square Publishers has years of experience and we aim to use that knowledge and creative insight, alongside evolving technology, to reach the right readers for our books. From the ones who read a lot, to the ones who don't consider themselves readers, we aim to find those who will love our books and talk about them as much as we do.

We are hunting for vital new voices from all backgrounds – with books that take the reader to new places and transform perceptions of the world we live in.

Follow us on social media for the latest Bedford Square Publishers news.

🐦 @bedsqpublishers
facebook.com/bedfordsq.publishers/
@bedfordsq.publishers

https://bedfordsquarepublishers.co.uk/